I0355514

# How to Trade in Stocks

*His own words: The Jesse Livermore
secret trading formula for understanding
timing, money management, and emotional control*

## Jesse Livermore

Added material by:

**Richard Smitten**

**McGraw-Hill**

New York   Chicago   San Francisco   Lisbon   London
Madrid   Mexico City   Milan   New Delhi   San Juan
Seoul   Singapore   Sydney   Toronto

The *McGraw·Hill* Companies

Copyright © 2001 by Richard Smitten. All rights reserved. Printed in the United States of America. Except as permitted under the United States Copyright Act of 1976, no part of this publication may be reproduced, stored in a retrieval system, or transmitted, in any form or by any means, electronic, mechanical, photocopying, recording, or otherwise, without the prior written permission of the publisher.

4 5 6 7 8 9 0    DOC/DOC    0 9 8 7

ISBN: 0-07-146979-6

This publication is designed to provide accurate and authoritative information with regard to the subject matter covered. It is sold with the understanding that the publisher is not engaged in rendering legal, accounting, or other professional advice. If legal advice or other expert assistance is required, the services of a competent professional person should be sought. —*From a declaration of principles jointly adopted by a committee of the American Bar Association and a committee of publishers.*

McGraw-Hill books are available at special discounts to use as premiums and sales promotions, or for use in corporate training programs. For more information, please write to the Director of Special Sales, Professional Publishing, McGraw-Hill, Two Penn Plaza, New York, NY 10121-2298. Or contact your local bookstore.

# Table of Contents

Timing—Understanding Industry Group Action
(TDT) Top Down Trading
(TT) Tandem Trading—Sister Stocks
(RPP) Understanding Reversal Pivotal Points
(CPP) Evaluating Continuation Pivotal Points
(S) Spikes
(ODR) One Day Reversals
(BONH) Breakout on a New High
(BOCB) Breakouts From a Consolidating Base
(V) Understand Volume
Stocks Have Personalities

## *Dedication*

This book is for my mother, Frankie Smitten. A woman of great courage, patience and wisdom...a great human being.

My mother adds the final ingredient, her great love.

Richard Smitten

## Special Thanks

I would like to thank Patricia Livermore and Paul Livermore for their kind help and counsel in writing this book. I would also like to officially thank my father, Louis Smitten for all his expert help. And my best friend Gordon Badger for his always sage advice on all subjects.

Teresa Darty Alligood deserves the strongest "thank you" for her great job of single-handedly producing and editing the book. She also designed the cover, which I think is outstanding.

And thanks to Edward Dobson, president and publisher of **Traders Press, Inc.®** for his unyielding belief in Jesse Livermore and his methods of trading the market. We both concur that Jesse Livermore was a stock market "Master" who can teach us much about the markets of today.

And most importantly to Jesse Livermore for originally writing this great book in 1940, a book that is just as valid today as the day it was written.

> *"Wall Street never changes, the pockets change,*
> *the stocks change, but Wall Street never changes,*
> *because human nature never changes."*
> —**Jesse Livermore**

Thank you Jesse Livermore, for your wisdom, hard work, and your high intelligence. And your never ending quest to learn the ways of the stock market.

Richard Smitten

# INTRODUCTION

## MEET THE LEGENDARY JESSE LIVERMORE

This classic book, *How To Trade in Stocks,* was written by Jesse Livermore, and is in his original words, with additional comments and updates by Richard Smitten.

In this book, there are numerous secrets revealed on Livermore's trading techniques, never before disclosed. The secrets come from extensive interviews with the Livermore family, Livermore's private papers, and intimate conversations with Paul Livermore, Livermore's son, who had never before spoken of his father. These personal insights were invaluable in understanding Jesse Livermore the man, and the trader.

In every human field of endeavor there are only a few individuals who tower over other men and women: Albert Einstein, Henry Ford, Thomas Edison, Louis Pasteur, Madame Curie; in athletics—Babe Ruth, Michael Jordan and Tiger Woods. Why does the individual often succeed in making landmark breakthroughs, and not the group. This remains an unanswered mystery.

Jesse Livermore was such a man, a leader in his field. Why is he not better known beyond Wall Street? Because he was a loner, a silent and secretive person. He had learned the power of silence and the power of keeping his actions secret. Throughout his career, he had often been hurt by revealing his secrets and hurt when he broke his code of silence...he paid the price on many occasions. He told his sons that the only time he seriously lost money was when he listened to other people.

His secretiveness and silence was legend on Wall Street and it only made the media hungrier in trying to get him to comment-to talk to them about his business. He was a media darling. He often refused to comment on the market, but the press would somehow find a story, even if they had to manufacture it out of rumors and innuendoes.

When the market was volatile, Livermore was the man everyone wanted to hear from. He was a legend on Wall Street. When he was fifteen, he started with his first trade of $3.12 and he was a millionaire before he was thirty. He called the great market crash of 1907, where he made three million dollars in a single day. In that crash J.P. Morgan, after he financed the brokers, to save them from bankruptcy sent a special envoy to beg Livermore to stop shorting the market.

He cornered entire commodity markets: cotton, corn, wheat, where he actually owned every bale or bushel in existence in the United States.

He was able to call market tops; he went short the 1929 crash and made a hundred million dollars in profit.

But he worked hard for his good fortune. As a boy of fourteen he kept a notebook with thousands of trades penciled in. He found patterns and trends, and practiced theories of his own and others.

## TRADE LIKE JESSE LIVERMORE

A software package will be available very soon to help people to trade using the Jesse Livermore methodology. Inside this software package there will be an instructional "VIRTUAL STOCK MARKET COMPUTER SIMULATOR" to allow the trader to apply Livermore's trading techniques and methods with no financial risk. Once a trader has progressed and gets mastery over the "Virtual Stock Market Computer Simulator" they can move to the other side of the software and actually trade for real. This virtual stock market simulator is designed for both the seasoned trader as well as the novice.

And as he said to Paul his son: "Perhaps by reading of my mistakes and shortcomings you will be able to avoid the pitfalls that wait and befall every active trader and speculator. Learn through my mistakes and my victories in the market and you will prosper." Be sure to read both of these great books for a complete study on Jesse Livermore.

Why numerical and chart formations repeat themselves is unknown. Livermore explained it away to human nature:

*"All through time, people have basically acted and re-acted the same way in the market as a result of: greed, fear, ignorance, and hope— that is why the numerical formations and patterns recur on a constant basis."*     **—Jesse Livermore**

Richard Smitten

# LIVERMORE'S NEW YEAR'S RITUAL

"Good afternoon, Mr. Livermore."

"Hello Alfred."

It was the Friday before New Year's of 1923. Livermore walked into the Chase Manhattan Bank, late in the afternoon. He was warmly greeted by Alfred Pierce, the bank manager. Livermore was one of the bank's best customers keeping a balance of at least two million dollars in reserve for his special "market situations," where he needed extra cash to establish one of his famous stock purchases or perhaps engage in a raid or a commodity corner.

"We have everything ready for you, J.L." Alfred said.

Livermore looked at his watch it was almost five-fifteen The bank was already closed. They had let him enter the bank through the employee's door.

"Yes, J.L., the closing bank vault time-lock is set for five thirty, as always."

They walked in silence across the great vaulted room of the main branch through the door that separated the tellers cages from the public and entered the back of the bank.

"And Monday morning?" Livermore asked.

"Monday, the timer on the vault is set to open at eight sharp, like always."

"I just like to be sure." Livermore added.

"I understand, J.L.—by that time you will have had enough solitude."

"Yes Alfred, of that I am sure." Livermore said. He was carrying a leather briefcase.

Alfred looked at the briefcase. "Do you mind me asking what's in the briefcase?"

"Not at all. It is my entire trading history for 1923. I will review every trade I made and refer to my notes. I keep good notes on all my trades that explain why I bought or went short and why I closed my positions."

"So you don't win every time?" Alfred said facetiously.

"Alfred there are many rumors about me, of course you know that I lose. I am only human. The idea is to get out fast when a trade goes against you. I often lose, that is what I am trying to figure out this weekend–why did I lose on certain trades over the year."

They approached the main vault. It was huge with a giant solid steel door. Two armed security men stood on either side of the door. They nodded at Alfred and Jesse Livermore. They knew what was going on.

Livermore and the bank manager crossed over the threshold and entered the cavernous vault. There was a large amount of cash sitting in a series of chests. Most of the bills were hundreds with one chest full of twenties and fifties. There was a desk, a chair, a cot, and an easy chair in the middle of the cash. There was a special light above the desk and a second light above the easy chair.

Livermore went over to the cash in the open chests and looked down at the uncovered bills.

"J.L. there is almost fifty million here. The exact amount is written on the pad on the desk. The last of it came over from E.F. Hutton's this afternoon."

Jesse Livermore had sold out almost every position he had in both stocks and commodities, as he did at the beginning of every new year. He stared down at the cash.

"I would like to have the commission on just these sales, J.L.," Alfred said.

"This is not all of it. In some cases the market was too thin to take the hit, so that stock will be sold over the next few weeks or so with a few exceptions, and will be sent here for safekeeping."

"When will you resume trading?"

"Most likely in February, after I get to Palm Beach."

The red light on the ceiling started to flash and a low level bell rang at twenty second intervals. The bank manager looked at his watch.

"Five minutes before the vault closes, J.L.. The food is over here." The bank manager went to an icebox in the corner. "We got everything that your office manager Harry Dache', ordered for you. He actually brought the food over himself about an hour ago and we had an ice delivery around noon. Bread, cold cuts, vegetables, water, milk, juices and the makings for some old fashioneds." Alfred pointed into the open ice-box door.

"Thanks, those old fashioneds will come in handy."

"Right you are, J.L.. I'm going to leave now, I suffer from claustrophobia and all this money scares me."

Livermore walked the bank manager to the vault door. They shook hands. "J.L. if anyone ever knew about this, they might think you were eccentric."

"Eccentric is a kind word, Alfred." Jesse Livermore smiled as the door started to swing shut, pushed by the two armed guards.

Livermore stood by the door as it clanged shut. The lights above the desk and the easy chair now provided an eerie hue. Livermore surmised that no one had ever actually tested them with the door shut, no one would volunteer to be locked inside the vault.

He turned and walked to the desk surrounded by almost fifty million dollars in cash. For the next two days and three nights this would be his home. Inside the cavernous vault he would retreat into deep solitude and review his year from every aspect...just as he had done every year since he got rich.

When it was time to leave on Monday morning he would go to the chest that held the twenties and the fifties and stuff his pockets with as much cash as he desired and over the next two weeks he would spend that cash.

He had not locked himself up with his cash as a miser might lock himself up to count his money in the counting house. No, Livermore, because his world was a world of paper transactions all year long, believed that by the end of the year he had lost his perception about what the paper slips really represented, cash money and ultimately power.

By the end of the year he was just shuffling paper. Livermore needed to touch the money and feel the power of cash. It also made him re-appraise his stock and commodity positions and re-appraise these positions and determine if these were positions he would keep if he had the choice–were there better opportunities.

When he walked out of the vault on the Monday morning he started his shopping spree, a spree that usually lasted for at least a week.

THE SECRET LIVERMORE MARKET KEY, EXACTLY AS PRINTED IN THE 1940 EDITION, IS AT THE REAR OF THE BOOK.

NOTE: THE FOLLOWING TEXT IS A WORD FOR WORD TRANSCRIPTION OF THE ORIGINAL LIVERMORE TEXT.

## Chapter 1 - LIVERMORE SPEAKS

# CHALLENGE OF SPECULATION

THE game of speculation is the most uniformly fascinating game in the world. But it is not a game for the stupid, the mentally lazy, the man of inferior emotional balance, or for the get-rich-quick adventurer. They will die poor.

Over a long period of years I have rarely attended a dinner party including strangers, that someone did not sit down beside me and after the usual pleasantries inquire:

"How can I make some money in the market?"

In my younger days I would go to considerable pains to explain all the difficulties faced by the one who simply wishes to take quick and easy money out of the market; or through courteous evasiveness I would work my way out of the snare.

In later years my answer has been a blunt "I don't know."

It is difficult to exercise patience with such people. In the first place, the inquiry is not a compliment to the man who has made a scientific study of investment and speculation. It would be as fair for the layman to ask an attorney or a surgeon:

"How can I make some quick money in law or surgery?"

I have come to the conviction, however, that larger numbers of people interested in stock-market investment and speculation would be willing to work and study to attain sensible results, if they had a guide or signpost pointing them in the right direction. And it is for them that this book is written. It is my purpose to include some of the highlights of a lifetime of speculative experience—a record of some of the failures and successes and the lessons that each has taught. Out of it all emerges my theory of "time element" in trading, which I regard as the most important factor in successful speculation.

But before we go any further, let me warn you that the fruits of your success will be in direct ratio to the honesty and sincerity of your own effort in keeping your own records, doing your own thinking, and reaching your own conclusions.

You cannot wisely read a book on "How to keep fit" and leave the physical exercises to another. Nor can you delegate to another the task of keeping your records, if you are to follow faithfully my formula for combining Timing, Money Management, and Emotional Control, as set forth in subsequent pages. I can only light the way, and I shall be happy, if through my guidance, you are able to take more money out of the stock market than you put in.

In this book, I present to that portion of the public, which at times may be speculatively inclined, some points and ideas which have been garnered during my many years as an investor and speculator. Anyone who is inclined to speculate should look at speculation as a *"business"* and treat it as such and not regard it as a pure gamble as so many people are apt to do.

If I am correct in the premise that speculation is a business in itself, those engaging in that business should be determined to learn and understand it to the best of their ability with informative data available. In the forty years, which I have devoted to making speculation a successful business venture, I have discovered and am still discovering new rules to apply to that business.

On many occasions I have gone to bed wondering why I had not been able to foresee a certain imminent move, and awakened in the early hours of the ensuing morning with a new idea formulated. I was impatient for the morning to arrive in order to start checking over my records of past movements to determine whether the new idea had merit. In most cases it was far from being 100% right, but what good there was in it was stored away in my subconscious mind. Perhaps, later, another idea would take form and I would immediately set to work checking it over.

In time these various ideas began to crystallize and I was able to develop a concrete method of keeping records in such a form that I could use them as a guide.

My theory and practical application have proved to my satisfaction that nothing new ever occurs in the business of speculating or investing in securities or commodities. There are times when one should speculate, and just as surely there are times when one should not speculate.

There is a very true adage: *"You can beat a horse race, but you can't beat the races."* So it is with market operations. There are times when money can be made investing and speculating in stocks, but money cannot consistently be made trading every day or every week during the year. Only the foolhardy will try it. It just is not in the cards and cannot be done.

To invest or speculate successfully, one must form an opinion as to what the next move of importance will be in a given stock. Speculation is nothing more than anticipating coming movements. In order to anticipate correctly, one must have a definite basis for that anticipation, but one has to be careful because people are often not predictable—they are full of emotion—and the market is made up of people. The good speculators always wait and have patience, waiting for the market to confirm their judgment. For instance, analyze in your own mind the effect, marketwise, that a certain piece of news which has been made public may have in relation to the market. Try to anticipate the psychological effect of this particular item on the market. If you believe it likely to have a definite bullish or bearish effect marketwise, don't back your judgment *"UNTIL THE ACTION OF THE MARKET ITSELF CONFIRMS YOUR OPINION."* The effect marketwise may not be as pronounced as you are inclined to believe it should be. Do not anticipate and move without market confirmation—being a little late in your trade is your insurance that you are right or wrong.

To illustrate further: After the market has been in a definite trend for a given period, a bullish or bearish piece of news may not have the slightest effect on the market, or it may have a temporary effect... the market itself at the time may be in an overbought or oversold condition, in which case the effect of that particular news would certainly be ignored. At such times the recording value of past performances under similar conditions becomes of inestimable value to the investor or speculator.

At such times you must entirely ignore personal opinion and apply strict attention to the action of the market itself. *"Markets are never wrong—opinions often are."*

The latter are of no value to the investor or speculator unless the market acts in accordance with his ideas.

Timing—No one man, or group of men, can make or break a

market today. One may form an opinion regarding a certain stock and believe that it is going to have a pronounced move, either up or down, and eventually be correct in his opinion but will lose money by presuming or acting on his opinion too soon. Believing it to be right, he acts immediately, only to find that after he has made his commitment, the stock goes the other way. The market becomes narrow; he becomes tired and goes out. Perhaps a few days later it begins to look all right, and in he goes again, but no sooner has he re-entered it than it turns against him once more. Once more he begins to doubt his opinion and sells out. Finally the move starts up. Having been too hasty and having made two erroneous commitments, he loses courage. It is also likely that he has made other commitments and is not in a position to assume more. Thus, by the time the real move in the stock he jumped into prematurely is on, he is out of it.

The point I would emphasize here is that after forming an opinion with respect to a certain stock —do not be too anxious to get into it. Wait and watch the action of that stock for confirmation to buy. Have a fundamental basis to be guided by.

Say, for instance, a stock is selling around $25.00 and has been consolidating within a range of $22.00 to $28.00 for a considerable period. Assuming that you believe that the stock should eventually sell at $50.00, and it is $25.00 at the time, have patience and wait until the stock becomes active, until it makes a new high, at around $28-29. You will then know that marketwise you have been justified. The stock must have gone into a very strong position, or it would not have broken out. Having done so, it is altogether likely that it is starting a very definite advance—the move is on. That is the time for you to back your opinion. Don't let the fact that you did not buy at $25.00 cause you any aggravation. The chances are if you had, you would have become tired of waiting and would have been out of it when the move started, because having once gotten out at a lower price, you would have become disgruntled and would not have gone back in when you should have.

Experience has proved to me that the real money made in speculating has been: *"IN COMMITMENTS IN A STOCK OR COMMODITY SHOWING A PROFIT RIGHT FROM THE START."*

Later on, when some examples of my trading operations are given, you will notice I made my first trade at the psychological time that is, at a time where the force of the movement was so strong that it simply had to carry through. Not on my operation but because the force was so strong behind that particular stock. It simply had to and did go. There have been many times when I, like many other speculators, have not had the patience to await the sure thing. I wanted to have an interest at all times.

You may say: "With all your experience, why did you allow yourself to do so?" The answer to that is that I am human and subject to human weakness. Like all speculators, I permitted impatience to out-maneuver good judgment.

Speculation is very similar to playing a game of cards, whether it be poker, bridge or any similar game. Each of us is possessed with the common weakness of wanting to have an interest in every pot, and we certainly would like to play every hand at bridge. It is this human frailty which we all possess in some degree that becomes the investor's and speculators greatest enemy and will eventually, if not safeguarded, bring about his downfall.

It is a human trait to be "HOPEFUL" and equally so to be "FEARFUL," but when you inject hope and fear into the business of speculation, you are faced with a very formidable hazard, because you are apt to get the two confused and in reverse positions.

As an illustration: You buy a stock at $30.00. The next day it has a quick run-up to $32.00 or $32.50. You immediately become fearful that if you don't take the profit, the next day you may see it fade away—so out you go with a small profit, when that is the very time you should entertain all the hope in the world. Why should you worry about losing two points profit which you did not have the previous day? If you can make two points profit in one day, you might make two or three the next day, and perhaps five more the next week.

As long as a stock is acting right, and the market is right, do not be in a hurry to take a profit. You know you are right, because if you were not, you would have no profit at all. Let it ride and ride along with it. It may grow into a very large profit, and as long as the "action of the market does not give you any cause to worry," have the courage of your convictions and stay with it.

On the other hand, suppose you buy a stock at $30.00, and the next day it goes to $28.00, showing a two-point loss. You would not be fearful that the next day would possibly see a three-point loss or more. No, you would regard it merely as a temporary reaction, feeling certain that the next day it would recover its loss. But that is the time that you should be worried. That two-point loss could be followed by two points the next day, or possibly five or ten within the next week or two. That is when you should be fearful, because if you did not get out, you might be forced to take a much greater loss later on. That is the time you should protect yourself by selling your stock before the loss assumes larger proportions.

*"Profits always take care of themselves but losses never do."*

The speculator has to insure himself against considerable losses by taking the first small loss. In so doing, he keeps his account in order so that at some future time, when he has a constructive idea, he will be in a position to go into another deal, taking on the same amount of stock as he had when he was wrong.

The speculator has to be his own insurance broker, and the only way he can continue in business is to guard his capital account and never permit himself to lose enough to jeopardize his operations at some future date when his market judgment is correct.

While I believe that the successful investor or speculator must have well-advanced reasons for making commitments on either side of the market, I feel he must also be able, through some form of a specific guide, to determine when to make his first commitments.

Let me repeat, there are definitely certain times when a movement really gets under way, and I firmly believe that anyone who has the instinct of a speculator and has the patience, can devise a specific method to be used as a guide which will permit him to judge correctly when to make his initial commitment. Successful speculation is not a mere guess.

To be consistently successful, an investor or speculator must have rules to guide him. Certain guides that I utilize may be of no value to anyone else.

Why is that so? If they are of inestimable value to me, why should they not serve you equally well? The answer to that is: *"No guide can be 100% right."* If I use a certain guide, my own pet one, I know what should be the result. If my stock does not act as I anticipated, I immediately determine the time is not yet ripe—so I close out my commitment.

8

Perhaps a few days later my guide indicates I should get in again, so back I go, and probably this time it is 100% correct. I believe anyone who will take the time and trouble to study price movement should in time be able to develop a guide, which will aid him in future operations or investments. In this book I present some points which I have found valuable in my own speculative operations.

A great many traders keep charts or records of averages. They chase them around, up and down, and there is no question that these charts of averages do point out a definite trend at times. Personally, charts have never appealed to me. I think they are altogether too confusing. Nevertheless, I am just as much of a fanatic in keeping records as other people are in maintaining charts. They may be right, and I may be wrong.

My preference for records is due to the fact that my recording method gives me a clear picture of what is happening. But it was not until I began to take into consideration the time element that my records really became useful in helping me to anticipate coming movements of importance. I believe that by keeping proper records and taking the time element into consideration—and I shall explain this in detail later—"one can with a fair degree of accuracy forecast coming movements of importance." But it takes patience to do so.

Familiarize yourself with a stock, or different groups of stocks, and if you figure the timing element correctly in conjunction with your records, sooner or later you will be able to determine when a major move is due. If you read your records correctly, you can pick the leading stock in any group. You must, I repeat, keep your own records. You must put down your own figures. Don't let anyone else do it for you. You will be surprised how many new ideas you will formulate in so doing; ideas which no one else could give you, because they are your discovery, your secret, and you should keep them your secret.

I offer in this book some DON'T'S" for investors and speculators. One of the primary "DON'T'S" is—one should never permit speculative ventures to run into investments. Don't become an *"Involuntary Investor."* Investors often take tremendous losses for no other reason than that their stocks are bought and paid for.

How often have you heard an investor say: "I don't have to worry about fluctuations or margin calls. I never speculate. When I buy stocks, I buy them for an investment, and if they go down, eventually they will come back."

But unhappily for such investors many stocks bought at a time when they were deemed good investments have later met with drastically changed conditions. Hence such so-called "investment stocks" frequently become purely speculative. Some go out of existence altogether. The original "investment" evaporates into thin air along with the capital of the investor. This occurrence is due to the failure to realize that so-called "investments" may be called upon in the future to face a new set of conditions that would jeopardize the earning capacity of the stock, originally bought for a permanent investment.

Before the investor learns of this changed situation, the value of his investment is already greatly depreciated. Therefore the investor must guard his capital account just as the successful speculator does in his speculative ventures. If this were done, those who like to call themselves "investors" would not be forced to become unwilling speculators of the future—nor would trust fund accounts depreciate so much in their value.

You will recall not so many years ago it was considered safer to have your money invested in the New York, New Haven & Hartford Railroad than to have it in a bank. On April 23, 1902, New Haven was selling at $255 a share. In December of 1906, Chicago, Milwaukee & St. Paul sold at $199.62. In January of that same year Chicago Northwestern sold at $240 a share. On February 9 of that year Great Northern Railway sold at $348 a share. All were paying good dividends.

Look at those "investments" today: On January 2, 1940, they were quoted at the following prices: New York, New Haven & Hartford Railroad $.50 per share; Chicago Northwestern at 5/16, which is about $.31 per share. On January 2, 1940, there was no quotation for Chicago, Milwaukee & St. Paul—but on January 5, 1940, it was quoted at $.25 per share.

It would be simple to run down the list of hundreds of stocks which, in my time, have been considered gilt-edge investments, and which today are worth little or nothing. Thus, great investments tumble, and with them the fortunes of so-called conservative investors in the continuous distribution of wealth.

Speculators in stock markets have lost money. But I believe it is a safe statement that the money lost by speculation alone is small compared with the gigantic sums lost by so-called investors who have let their investments ride.

From my viewpoint, the investors are the big gamblers. They make a bet, stay with it, and if it goes wrong, they lose it all. The speculator might buy at the same time. But if he is an intelligent speculator, he will recognize—if he keeps records—the danger signal warning him all is not well. He will, by acting promptly, hold his losses to a minimum and await a more favorable opportunity to reenter the market.

When a stock starts sliding downward, no one can tell how far it will go. Nor can anyone guess the ultimate top on a stock in a broad upward movement. A few thoughts should be kept uppermost in mind.

One should  never sell a stock, because it seems high-priced. You may watch the stock go from 10 to 50 and decide that it is selling at too high a level. That is the time to determine what is to prevent it from starting at 50 and going to 150 under favorable earning conditions and good corporate management. Many have lost their capital funds by selling a stock short after a long upward movement, when it "seemed too high."

Conversely, never buy a stock because it has had a big decline from its previous high. The likelihood is that the decline is based on a very good reason. That stock may still be selling at an extremely high price relative to its value—even if the current level seems low.

Try to forget its past high range and study it on the basis of the formula that combines timing and money management.

It may surprise many to know that in my method of trading, when I see by my records that an upward trend is in progress, I become a buyer as soon as a stock makes a *"new high on its movement, after having had a normal reaction."*

The same applies whenever I take the short side. Why? Because I am following the trend at the time. My records signal me to go ahead!

I never buy on reactions or go short on rallies.

One other point: *"It is foolhardy to make a second trade, if your first trade shows you a loss."*

*"Never average losses."* Let that thought be written indelibly upon your mind.

## Chapter 2 - LIVERMORE SPEAKS

# WHEN DOES A STOCK ACT RIGHT?

STOCKS, like individuals, have a character and a personality. Some are high-strung, nervous, and jumpy—others are forthright, direct, logical. A skillful trader comes to know and respect individual securities. Their action is predictable under varying sets of conditions. Markets never stand still. They are very dull at times, but they are not resting at one price. They are either moving up or down a fraction.

When a stock gets into a definite trend, it works automatically and consistently along certain lines throughout the progress of its move.

At the beginning of the move you will notice a very large volume of sales with gradually advancing prices for a few days. Then what I term a "Normal Reaction" will occur. On that reaction the sales volume will be much less than on the previous days of its advance.

Now that little reaction is only normal. Never be afraid of the normal movement. But be very fearful of abnormal movements, like a major change in personality.

In a day or two activity will start again, and the volume will increase. If it is a real movement, in a short space of time the natural, normal reaction will have been recovered, and the stock will be selling in new high territory. That movement should continue strong for a few days with only minor daily reactions.

Sooner or later it will reach a point where it is due for another normal reaction. When it occurs, it should be on the same lines as the first reaction, because that is the natural way any stock will act when it is in a definite trend.

At the first part of a movement of this kind the distance above the previous high point to the next high point is not very great. But as time goes on you will notice that it is making much faster headway on the upside.

Let me illustrate: Take a stock that starts at 50. On the first leg of the movement it might gradually sell up to 54. A day or two of normal reaction might carry it back to 52. Three days later it is on its way again. In that time it might go up to 59 or 60 before the normal reaction would occur.

But instead of reacting, say, only a point or a point and one-half, a natural reaction from that level could easily be 3 points. When it resumes its advance again in a few days, you will notice that the volume of sales at that time is not nearly as large as it was at the beginning of the move.

The stock is becoming harder to buy.

That being the case, the next points in the movement will be much more rapid than before. The stock could easily go *from* the previous high of 60 to 68 or 70 without encountering a natural reaction.

When that normal reaction does occur, it could be more severe. It could easily react down to 65 and still have only a normal decline. But assuming that the reaction was five points or thereabouts, it should not be many days before the advance would be resumed, and the stock should be selling at a brand new high price. And that is where the "time element" comes in. Don't let the stock go stale on you. After attaining a goodly profit, you must have patience, but don't let patience create a frame of mind that ignores the danger signals.

The stock starts up again, and it has a rise of six or seven points in one day, followed the next day by perhaps eight to ten points—with great activity—but during the last hour of the day all of a sudden it has an abnormal break of seven or eight points. The next morning it extends its reaction another point or so, and then once more starts to advance, closing very strong. But the following day, for some reason, it does not carry through.

This is an immediate danger signal.

All during the progress of the move it had nothing but natural and normal reactions. Then all of a sudden an abnormal reaction occurs—and by "abnormal" I mean a reaction "in one day" of six or more points from an extreme price made in that same day —something it has not had before, and when something happens abnormally stock-marketwise, it is flashing you a danger signal which must not be ignored.

You have had patience to stay with the stock all during its natural progress. Now have the courage and good sense to honor the danger signal and step aside.

I do not say that these danger signals are always correct because, as stated before, no rules applying to stock fluctuations are 100% right. But if you pay attention to them consistently, in the long run you will profit immensely.

A speculator of great genius once told me:

"When I see a danger signal handed to me, I don't argue with it. I get out! A few days later, if everything looks all right, I can always go back in again. Thereby I have saved myself a lot of worry and money. I figure it out this way. If I were walking along a railroad track and saw an express train coming at me sixty miles an hour, I would be a damned fool not to get off the track and let the train go by. After it had passed, I could always get back on the track again, if I desired. I have always remembered that as a graphic bit of speculative wisdom.

Every judicious speculator is on the alert for danger signals.

Curiously, the trouble with most speculators is that something inside of them keeps them from mustering enough courage to close out their commitment when they should. They hesitate and during that period of hesitation they watch the market go many points against them. Then they say: "On the next rally I'll get out!" When the next rally comes, as it will eventually, they forget what they intended to do, because in their opinion the market is acting fine again. However, that rally was only a temporary swing that soon plays out, and then the market starts to go down in earnest. And they are in it—due to their hesitation. If they had been using a guide, it would have told them what to do; not only saving them a lot of money but eliminating their worries.

Again let me say, the human side of every person is the greatest enemy of the average investor or speculator. Why shouldn't a stock rally after it starts down from a big advance? Of course it will rally from some level. But why hope it is going to rally at just the time you want it to rally? Chances are it won't, and if it does, the vacillating type of speculator may not take advantage of it.

What I am trying to make clear to that part of the public which desires to regard speculation as a serious business, and I wish deliberately to reiterate it, is that wishful thinking must be banished; that one cannot be successful by speculating every day or every week; that there are only a few times a year, possibly four or five, when you should allow yourself to make any commitment at all. In the interims you are letting the market shape itself for the next big movement. If you have timed the movement correctly, your first commitment will show you a profit at the start. From then on, all that is required of you is to be alert, watching for the appearance of the danger signal to tell you to step aside and convert paper profits into real money.

Remember this: When you are doing nothing, those speculators who feel they must trade day in and day out, are laying the foundation for your next venture. You will reap benefits from their mistakes.

Speculation is far too exciting. Most people who speculate hound the brokerage offices or receive frequent telephone calls, and after the business day they talk markets with friends at all gatherings. The ticker or translux is always on their minds. They are so engrossed with the minor ups and downs that they miss the big movements.

Almost invariably the vast majority have commitments on the wrong side when the broad trend swings under way. The speculator who insists on trying to profit from daily minor movements will never be in a position to take advantage of the next important change marketwise when it occurs.

Such weaknesses can be corrected by keeping and studying records of stock price movements and how they occur, and by taking the time element carefully into account.

Many years ago I heard of a remarkably successful speculator who lived in the California mountains and received quotations three days old. Two or three times a year he would call on his San Francisco broker and begin writing out orders to buy or sell, depending upon his market position. A friend of mine, who spent time in the broker's office, became curious and made inquiries. His astonishment mounted when he learned of the man's extreme detachment from market facilities, his rare visits, and, on occasions, his tremendous volume of trade.

Finally he was introduced, and in the course of conversation inquired of this man from the mountains how he could keep track of the stock market at such an isolated distance.

"Well," the man replied, "I make speculation a business. I would be a failure if I were in the confusion of things and let myself be distracted by minor changes. I like to be away where I can think. You see, I keep a record of what has happened, after it has happened, and it gives me a rather clear picture of what markets are doing.

"Real movements do not end the day they start. It takes time to complete the end of a genuine movement. By being up in the mountains I am in a position to give these movements all the time they need. But a day comes when I get some prices out of the paper and put them down in my records. I notice the prices I record are not conforming to the same pattern of movements that has been apparent for some time.

"Right then I make up my mind. I go to town and get busy!"

That happened many years ago. Consistently, the man from the mountains, over a long period of time, drew funds abundantly from the stock market. He was something of an inspiration to me. I went to work harder than ever trying to blend the "time element" with all the other data I had compiled. By constant effort I was able to bring my records into a co-ordination that aided me to a surprising degree in anticipating coming movements.

## Chapter 3 - LIVERMORE SPEAKS

# FOLLOW THE LEADERS

THERE is always the temptation in the stock market, after a period of success, to become careless or excessively ambitious. Then it requires sound common sense and clear thinking to keep what you have. But it is not necessary to lose your money, once you have acquired it, if you will hold fast to sound principles.

We know that prices move up and down. They always have and they always will.

My theory is that: *"Behind these major movements is an irresistible force."*

That is all one needs to know. It is not good to be too curious about all the reasons behind price movements. You risk the danger of clouding your mind with non-essentials. Just recognize that the movement is there and take advantage of it by steering your speculative ship along with the tide. Do not argue with the condition, and most of all, do not try to combat it.

Remember too that it is dangerous to start spreading out all over the market. By this I mean, do not have an *"Interest in too many stocks at one time. It is much easier to watch a few than many."* I made that mistake years ago and it cost me money.

Another mistake I made was to permit myself to turn completely bearish or bullish on the whole market, because one stock in some particular group had plainly reversed its course from the general market trend. Before making a new commitment, I should have been patient and awaited the time, when some stock in another group had indicated to me that its decline or advance had ended. In time, other stocks would clearly give the same indication. Those are the cues I should have waited for.

But instead of doing so, I felt the costly urge of getting busy in the whole market. Thus I permitted the hankering for activity to replace common sense and judgment. Of course I made money on my trades in the first and second groups. But I chipped away a substantial part of it by entering other groups before the zero hour had arrived.

Back in the wild bull markets of the late twenties I saw clearly that the advance in the copper stocks had come to an end. A short time later the advance in the motor group reached its zenith. Because the bull market in those two groups had terminated, I soon arrived at the faulty conclusion that I could safely sell everything. I should hate to tell you the amount of money I lost by acting upon that premise.

While I was piling up huge paper profits on my copper and motor deals, I lost even more in the next six months trying to find the top of the utility group. Eventually this and other groups reached their peaks. By that time Anaconda was selling 50 points below its previous high and the motor stocks in about the same ratio.

What I wish to impress upon you is the fact that when you clearly see a move coming in a particular group, act upon it. But do not let yourself act in the same way in some other group, until you plainly see signs that the second group is in a position to follow suit. Have patience and wait. In time you will get the same tip-off in other groups that you received in the first group. Just don't spread out over the market.

Confine your studies of movements to the prominent stocks of the day. If you cannot make money out of the leading active issues, you are not going to make money out of the stock market as a whole.

Just as styles in women's gowns and hats and costume jewelry are forever changing with time, the old leaders of the stock market are dropped and new ones rise up to take their places. Years ago the chief leaders were the railroads, American Sugar, and Tobacco. Then came the steels, and American Sugar and Tobacco were nudged into the background. Then came the motors, and so on up to the present time.

Today, in 1940, we have only four groups in the position of dominating the market: steels, motors, aircraft stocks, and mail orders. As they go, so goes the whole market. In the course of time new leaders will come to the front; some of the old leaders will be dropped.

It will always be that way as long as there is a stock market.

Definitely it is not safe to try to keep account of too many stocks at one time. You will become entangled and confused. Try to analyze comparatively few groups. You will find it is much easier to obtain a true picture that way than if you tried to dissect the whole market.

If you analyze correctly the course of two stocks in the four prominent groups, you need not worry about what the rest are going to do. It becomes the old story of "follow the leader." Keep mentally flexible. Remember the leaders of today may not be the leaders two years from now.

Today, in my records I keep four individual groups. That does not mean I am trading in all of the groups at the same time. But I have a genuine purpose in mind.

When I first became interested in the movement of prices long,

long ago when I was 15 years old, I decided to test my ability to anticipate correctly forthcoming movements.

I recorded fictitious trades in a little book that was always with me. In the course of time, I made my first actual trade. I never will forget that trade. I had half-interest in a purchase of five shares of Chicago, Burlington & Quincy Railway Stock, bought with a friend of mine, and my share of the profit amounted to $3.12. From that time on I became a speculator on my own.

Under conditions as they currently exist, I do not believe that a speculator of the old type who traded in huge volume has much chance of success. When I say a speculator of the old type, I am thinking of the days when markets were very broad and liquid and when a speculator might take a position with 5,000 or 10,000 shares of a stock and move in and out without greatly influencing the price.

After taking his initial position, if the stock acted right, the speculator could safely add to his line from that time forward. In former times, if his judgment proved faulty, he could move out of his position easily without taking too serious a loss. But today, if his first position proved untenable, he would suffer a devastating loss in changing about because of the comparative narrowness of the market.

On the other hand, as I have implied previously, the speculator of today who has the patience and judgment to wait the proper time for acting has, in my opinion, a better chance of cashing in good profits eventually, because the current market does not lend itself to so many artificial movements, movements that far too frequently in the old days jarred all scientific calculations out of kilter.

It is obvious, therefore, that in light of conditions which exist today, no speculator who is intelligent will permit himself to operate on that scale which was more or less a commonplace some years ago. He will study a limited number of groups and of leaders in those groups. He will learn to look before he leaps. For a new age of markets has been ushered in—an age that offers safer opportunities for the reasonable, studious, competent investor and speculator.

## Chapter 4 - LIVERMORE SPEAKS

# MONEY IN THE HAND

WHEN you are handling surplus income do not delegate the task to anyone. Whether you are dealing in millions or in thousands the same principal lesson applies. It is your money. It will remain with you just so long as you guard it. Faulty speculation is one of the most certain ways of losing it.

Blunders by incompetent speculators cover a wide scale. I have warned against averaging losses. That is a most common practice. Great numbers of people will buy a stock, let us say at 50, and two or three days later if they can buy it at 47 they are seized with the urge to average down by buying another hundred shares, making an average price of 48 on all.

Having bought at 50 and being concerned over a three-point loss on a hundred shares, what rhyme or reason is there in adding another hundred shares and having the double worry when the price hits 44? At that point there would be a $600 loss on the first hundred shares and a $300 loss on the second hundred shares.

If one is to apply such an unsound principle, he should keep on averaging by buying two hundred shares at 44, then four hundred at 41, eight hundred at 38, sixteen hundred at 35, thirty-two hundred at 32, sixty-four hundred at 29 and so on. How many speculators could stand such pressure? Yet if the policy is sound it should not be abandoned. Of course abnormal moves such as the one indicated do not happen often. But it is just such abnormal moves against which the speculator must guard to avoid disaster.

So, at the risk of repetition and preaching, let me urge you to avoid averaging down. I know but one sure tip I got from a broker. It is your *"Margin Call—When the margin call reaches you, close your account—never meet a margin call."* You are on the wrong side of the market. Why send good money after bad? Keep that good money for another day. Risk it on something more attractive than an obviously losing deal.

A successful businessman extends credit to various customers but would not enjoy selling his entire output to one customer. The larger the number of customers the more widely the risk is spread. Just so, a person engaged in the business of speculation should risk only a limited amount of capital on any one venture. Cash to the speculator is as merchandise on the shelves of the merchant.

One major mistake of all speculators is the urge to enrich themselves in too short a time. Instead of taking two or three years to make 500% on their capital, they try to do it in two or three months. Now and then they succeed.

But do such daring traders keep it?

They do not. Why?

Because it is unhealthy money, rolling in rapidly, and stopping for but a short visit. The speculator in such instances loses his sense of balance. He says: "If I can make 500% on my capital in two months, think what I will do in the next two! I will make a fortune."

Such speculators are never satisfied. They continue to shoot the works until somewhere a cog slips, something happens—something drastic, unforeseen, and devastating. At length comes that final margin call from the broker, the call that cannot be met, and this type of plunger goes out like a lamp. He may plead with the broker for a little more time, or if he is not too unfortunate, he may have saved a nest egg permitting a modest new start.

Businessmen opening a shop or a store would not expect to make over 25% on their investment the first year. But to people who enter the speculative field 25% is nothing. They are looking for 100%. And their calculations are faulty; they fail to make speculation a business and run it on business principles. Here is another little point that might well be remembered. A speculator should make it a rule each time he closes out a successful deal to take one-half of his profits and lock this sum up in a safe deposit box. The only money that is ever taken out of Wall Street by speculators is the money they draw out of their accounts after closing a successful deal.

I recall one day in Palm Beach. I left New York with a fairly large short position open. A few days after my arrival in Palm Beach the market had a severe break. That was an opportunity to cash "paper profits" into real money—and I did.

After the market closed I gave a message to the telegraph operator to tell the New York office to send immediately to my bank one million dollars to be deposited to my credit. The telegraph operator almost passed out. After sending the message, he asked if he might keep that slip. I inquired why.

He said: "I've been an operator here in Palm Beach for twenty years and that was the first message I ever sent asking a broker to deposit money in a bank account of a customer."

He went on: "I've seen thousands and thousands of messages passing over the wire from brokers demanding margins from customers. But never before one like yours. I want to show it to the boys."

The only time the average speculator can draw money from his brokerage account is when he has no position open or when he has an excessive equity. He won't draw it out when the markets are going against him because he needs all his capital for margin.

He won't draw it out after closing a successful deal because he says to himself: "Next time I'll make twice as much."

Consequently most speculators rarely see the money. To them the money is nothing real, nothing tangible. For years, after a successful deal was closed, I made it a habit to draw out cash. I used to draw it out at the rate of $200,000 or $300,000 a clip. It is a good policy. It has a psychological value. Make it a policy to do that. Count the money over. I did. I knew I had something in my hand. I felt it. It was real.

Money in a broker's account or in a bank account is not the same as if you feel it in your own fingers once in a while. Then it means something. There is a sense of possession that makes you just a little bit less inclined to take headstrong chances of losing your gains. So have a look at your real money once in a while, particularly between your market deals.

There is too much looseness in these matters on the part of the average speculator. When a speculator is fortunate enough to double his original capital he should at once draw out one half of his profit to be set-aside for reserve. This policy has been tremendously helpful to me on many occasions. I only regret that I have not observed it throughout my career. In some places it would have smoothed the path.

I never have been able to make a dollar outside of Wall Street.

But I have lost many millions of dollars, which I had taken from Wall Street, "investing" in other ventures. I have in mind real estate in the Florida boom, oil wells, airplane manufacturing, and the perfecting and marketing of products based on new inventions. Always I lost every cent.

In one of these outside ventures that had whipped up my enthusiasm I sought to interest a friend of mine to the extent of $50,000. He listened to my story very attentively. When I had finished he said: "Livermore, you will never make a success in any business outside of your own. Now if you want $50,000 with which to speculate it is yours for the asking. But please speculate and stay away from business." Next morning, to my surprise, the mail brought a check for that amount which I did not need.

The lesson here again is that speculation itself is a business and should be so viewed by all. Do not permit yourself to be influenced by excitement, flattery or temptation. Keep in mind that brokers sometimes innocently become the undoing of many speculators. Brokers are in the business to make commissions. They cannot make commissions unless customers trade. The more trade, the more commissions. The speculator wants to trade and the broker not only is willing but too often encourages over-trading. The uninformed speculator regards the broker as his friend and is soon over-trading.

Now if the speculator were smart enough to know at just which time he should over-trade, the practice would be justified. He may know at times when he could or should over-trade. But once acquiring the habit, very few speculators are smart enough to stop. They are carried away, and they lose that peculiar sense of balance so essential to success. They never think of the day when they will be wrong. But that day arrives. The easy money takes wing, and another speculator is broke.

Never make any trade unless you know you can do so with financial safety.

## Chapter - 5 LIVERMORE SPEAKS

# THE PIVOTAL POINT

WHENEVER I have had the patience to wait for the market to arrive at what I call a "Pivotal Point" before I started to trade; I have always made money in my operations.

Why? Because I then commenced my play just at the psychological time at the beginning of a move. I never had a loss to worry about for the simple reason that I acted promptly and started to accumulate my line right at the time my personal guide told me to do so. All I had to co thereafter was just sit tight and let the market run its course, knowing if I did so, the action of the market itself would give me in due time the signal to take my profits.

And whenever I had the nerve and the patience to wait for the signal, it invariably did just that. It has always been my experience that I never benefited much from a move if I did not get in at somewhere near the beginning of that move. And the reason is that I missed the backlog of profit which is very necessary to provide the courage and patience to sit through a move until the end comes—and to stay through any minor reactions or rallies which were bound to occur from time to time before the movement had completed its course.

Just as markets in time will give you a positive tip when to get in—if you have patience to wait—they will just as surely give you a tip-off when to get out. "Rome was not built in a day," and no real movement of importance ends in one day or in one week. It takes time for it to run its logical course. It is significant that a large part of a market movement occurs in the last forty-eight hours of a play, and that is the most important time to be in it.

For example: Take a stock that has been in a Downward Trend for quite some time and reaches a low point of 40. Then it has a quick rally in a few days to 45, then it backs and fills for a week in a range of a few points, and then it starts to extend its rally until it reaches 49. The market becomes dull and inactive for a few days. Then one day it becomes active again and goes down 3 or 4 points, and keeps on going down until it reaches a price near its Pivotal Point of 40. Right here is the time the market should be watched carefully, because if the stock is really going to resume its Downward Trend in earnest it should sell below its Pivotal Point of 40 by three points or more before it has another rally of importance. If it fails to pierce 40 it is an indication to buy as soon as it rallies 3 points from the low price made on that reaction. If the 40 point has been pierced but not by the proper extent of 3 points, then it should be bought as soon as it advances to 43.

If either one of these two things happen, you will find, in the majority of cases, that it marks the beginning of a new trend, and if the trend is going to be confirmed in a positive manner, it will continue to advance and reach a price over the Pivotal point of 49—by 3 points or more.

I do not use the words "bullish" or "bearish" in defining trends of the market, because I think so many people, when they hear the words "bullish" or "bearish" spoken of marketwise immediately think that is the course the market is going to take for a very long time.

Well-defined trends of that kind do not occur very often—only once in about four or five years— but during that time there are many well-defined trends which last for a comparatively short time. I consequently use the words "Upward Trend" and "Downward Trend," because they fully express what is going on at that specific time. Moreover, if you make a purchase because you think the market is going into an Upward Trend, and then a few weeks later come to the conclusion the market is heading into a Downward Trend, you will find it much easier to accept the reversal in trend than if you had a confirmed opinion that the market was definitely in a "bullish" or "bearish" stage.

The Livermore Method, my method, of recording prices in conjunction with the "Timing, Money Management, and Emotional Control rules" is the result of over thirty years of study of principles that would serve me in forming a basic guide for the next important market movement.

After making my first record, I found it did not help me to any great extent. Weeks later I had a new thought that aroused me to fresh endeavors, only to find out that, while it was an improvement over the first one, it still did not give me the desired information. Successively new thoughts would come to mind, and I would make a set of new records.

Gradually, after making many of these, I began to develop ideas I did not have before, and each succeeding record I made began to shape itself into better form. But from the time I started to merge the time element with price movements, my records began to talk to me!

Each record thereafter I put together in a different way, and these eventually enabled me to ascertain Pivotal Points and in turn demonstrate how to use them profitably marketwise. I have changed my calculations since then a number of times, but these records today are set up in such a way that they can talk to you also—if you but let them.

When a speculator can determine the Pivotal Point of a stock and interpret the action at that point, he may make a commitment with the positive assurance of being right from the start.

Many years ago I began profiting from the simplest type of Pivotal Point trades. Frequently I had observed that when a stock sold at 50, 100, 200 and even 300, a fast and straight movement almost invariably occurred after such points were passed.

My first attempt to profit on these Pivotal Points was in the old Anaconda stock. The instant it sold at 100, I placed an order to buy 4,000 shares. The order was not completed until the stock crossed 105 a few minutes later. That day it sold up about ten points more and the next day had another remarkable bulge. With only a few normal reactions of seven or eight points the advance continued to well over 150 in a short period of time. At no time was the Pivotal Point of 100 in danger.

From then on I rarely missed a big play where there was a Pivotal Point on which to work. When Anaconda sold at 200, I repeated my successful play and did the same thing again when it sold at 300. But on that occasion it did not carry through to the proper extent. It sold only to 302 3/4. Plainly it was flashing the danger signal. So I sold out my 8,000 shares, being fortunate enough to receive 300 a share for 5,000 shares and 299 for 1,500 shares. The 6,500 shares were sold in less than two minutes. But it took twenty-five minutes more to sell the remaining 1,500 shares in 100 and 200 lots down to 298, where the stock closed.

I felt confident that if the stock broke below 300, it would have a swift downward move. Next morning there was excitement. Anaconda was way down in London, opened in New York substantially lower, and within a few days was selling at 225.

Bear in mind when using Pivotal Points in anticipating market movements, that if the stock does not perform as it should, after crossing the Pivotal Point, this is a danger signal that must be heeded.

As shown in the above incident, the action of Anaconda, after crossing 300, was entirely different than its action above 100 and 200, respectively. On those occasions there was a very fast advance of at least 10 to 15 points right after the Pivotal Point had been crossed. But this time, instead of the stock being hard to buy, the market was being supplied with quantities of it—to such an extent, the stock simply could not continue its advance. Therefore, the action of the stock right above 300 clearly showed it had become a dangerous stock to own. It clearly showed that what usually happens when a stock crosses its Pivotal Point was not going to be the case this time.

On another occasion I recall waiting three weeks before starting to buy Bethlehem Steel. On April 7, 1915, it had reached its highest price on record: 87. Having observed that stocks passing a Pivotal Point gained rapidly, and being confident that Bethlehem Steel would go through 100, on April 8 I placed my first order to buy and accumulated my line from 89 up to 99. The same day the stock sold up to a high of 117. It never halted in its upward flight except for minor reactions until April 13, or five days later, when it sold at a high of 155, a breath-taking rise. This again illustrates the rewards that go to the person who has the patience to wait for and take advantage of the Pivotal Points.

But I was not through with Bethlehem. I repeated the operation at the 200 point, at the 300 point, and again at the dizzy peak of 400. Nor had I finished even then, for I had anticipated what would happen in a bear market, when the stock broke the Pivotal Points on the way down. I learned the main thing was to watch the follow-through as it crossed through the Pivotal Point. I found it was an easy matter for me to turn around and get out of a position, when vitality was lacking after a stock crossed the Pivotal Point and there were many occasions when I reversed my position and went over to the short-side.

Incidentally, every time I lost patience and failed to await the Pivotal Points and fiddled around for some easy profits in the meantime, I would lose money.

Since those days there have been various splitups in shares of high-priced stocks and, accordingly, opportunities such as those I have just reviewed do not occur so often. Nevertheless, there are other ways by which one can determine Pivotal Points.

For instance, let us say that a new stock has been listed in the last two or three years and its high was 20, or any other figure, and that such a price was made two or three years ago. If something favorable happens in connection with the company, and the stock starts upward, usually it is a safe play to buy the minute it touches a brand-new high.

A stock may be brought out at 50, 60 or 70 a share, sell off 20 points or so, and then hold between the high and low for a year or two. Then if it ever sells below the previous low, that stock is likely to be in for a tremendous drop. Why? Because something must have gone wrong with the affairs of the company.

By keeping stock price records and taking into consideration the "time element," you will be able to find many Pivotal Points on which to make a commitment for a fast movement.

But to educate yourself to trade on these points requires patience. You must devote time to the study of records, made and entered in the record-book only by yourself, and in making notes at which prices the Pivotal Points will be reached. The results are almost beyond belief, the study of Pivotal Points is, you will find, a golden field for personal research.

You will derive from successful trades based on your own judgment a singular pleasure and satisfaction. You will discover that profits made in this way are immensely more gratifying than any which could possibly come from the tips or guidance of someone else. If you make your own discovery, trade your own way, exercise patience, and watch for the danger signals, you will develop a proper trend of thinking.

In the last chapters of this book I explain in detail my own method of determining the more complex Pivotal Points in conjunction with the Livermore Market Method.

Few people ever make money by trading on the occasional tips or recommendations of others. Many beg for information and then don't know how to use it.

At a dinner party one night a lady kept pestering me beyond endurance for some market advice. In one of those weak moments I told her to buy some Cerro de Pasco which that day had crossed a Pivotal Point. From the next morning's opening the stock advanced 15 points during the next week with only trifling reactions. Then the action of the stock gave forth a danger signal. I recalled the lady's inquiry and hastened to have Mrs. Livermore telephone her to sell.

Fancy my surprise to learn that she had not yet bought the stock as she first wanted to see whether my information was correct! So wags the world of market tips.

Commodities frequently offer attractive Pivotal Points. Cocoa is traded in on the New York Cocoa Exchange. During most years the movements in this commodity do not offer many speculative inducements. Nevertheless, in making speculation a business, one automatically keeps an eye on all markets for the big opportunities.

During the year 1934 the high price of the December option in Cocoa was made in February at 6.23, the low was made in October at 4.28. In 1935 the high price was made in February at 5.74, the low in June at 4.54. The low price in 1936 was made in March at 5.13. But in August of that year for some reason the Cocoa market became a very different market. Great activity developed. When Cocoa sold that month at a price of 6.88, it was far beyond the highest price of the previous two years and above its last two Pivotal Points.

In September it sold at a high of 7.51; in October the high was 8.70; in November it was 10.80; in December 11.40; and in January 1937 it made an extreme high of 12.86, having recorded a rise of 600 points in a period of five months with only a few minor normal reactions.

Obviously there was a very good reason for this rapid rise, as only normal movements occur year in and year out. The reason was a severe shortage in the supply of Cocoa. Those closely watching Pivotal Points found a splendid opportunity in the Cocoa market.

It is when you set down prices in your record book and observe the patterns that the prices begin to talk to you. All of a sudden you realize that the picture you are making is acquiring a certain form:

It is striving to make clear a situation that is building up.

It suggests that you go back over your records and see what the last movement of importance was under a similar set of conditions.

It is telling you that by careful analysis and good judgment you will be able to form an opinion.

The price pattern reminds you that every movement of importance is but a repetition of similar price movements, that just as soon as you familiarize yourself with the actions of the past, you will be able to anticipate and act correctly and profitably upon forthcoming movements I want to emphasize the fact, that: *I do not consider these records perfection, except as they serve me.*

I do know a basis is there for anticipating future movements and if anyone will study these records, keeping them themselves, they cannot fail to profit by it in their operations.

It would not surprise me if the persons who in the future follow my methods of keeping these records get even more out of them than I have. This statement is based on the premise that, whereas I arrived at my conclusions some time ago, as a result of my record analysis, those new people who begin to apply this method may very readily discover new points of value that I have missed.

I would further clarify this by stating that I have not looked for any further points, because, applying it as I have for some time past, it has entirely served my personal purpose. Someone else, however, may develop from this basic method new ideas which, when applied, will enhance the value of my basic method for their purpose.

If they are able to do so, you may rest assured that I will not be jealous of their success!

## Chapter 6 - LIVERMORE SPEAKS

# THE MILLION DOLLAR BLUNDER

IT is my purpose in these chapters to lay down some general trading principles. Later on there will be specific explanation of my formulas for combining Timing, Money Management and Emotional Control. In consideration of these general trading principles it should be said that too many speculators buy or sell impulsively, acquiring their entire line at almost one price. That is wrong and dangerous.

Let us suppose that you want to buy 500 shares of a stock. Start by buying 100 shares. Then if the market advances buy another 100 shares as a "probe" to see if your judgment is correct, and so on. But each succeeding purchase must be at a "higher price" than the previous one.

That same rule should be applied in selling short. Never make an additional sale unless it is at a lower price than the previous sale. By following this rule you will come nearer being on the right side than by any other method with which I am familiar. The reason for this procedure is that your trades have at all times shown you a profit. The fact that your trades "DO" show you a profit is proof you are right.

Under my trading practice you first would:

Size up the situation in regard to a particular stock.

Next it is important to determine at what price you should allow yourself to enter the market—the initial "BUY" point or "SELL" point if you are going short.

Study your book of price records, study carefully the movements of the past few weeks—looking for the Pivotal Point. When your chosen stock reaches the point you had previously decided it should reach if the move is going to start in earnest, that is the time to make your first commitment.

Having made that commitment, decide definitely the amount of money you are willing to risk should your calculations be wrong.

You may make one or two commitments on this theory and lose. But by being consistent and never failing to re-enter the market again whenever your Pivotal Point is reached, you cannot help but be in when the real move does occur. You simply cannot be out of it.

But careful timing is essential . . . impatience is costly. Let me tell you how I once missed a million-dollar profit through impatience and careless timing. I almost want to turn my face away in embarrassment when I tell this story.

Many years ago I became strongly bullish on Cotton. I had formed a definite opinion that Cotton was in for a big rise. But as frequently happens the market itself was not ready to start. No sooner had I reached my conclusion, however, than I had to poke my nose into Cotton.

My initial play was for 20,000 bales, purchased at the market. This order ran the dull market up fifteen points. Then, after my last 100 bales had been bought, the market proceeded to slip back in twenty-four hours to the price at which it had been selling when I started buying. There it slept for a number of days. Finally, in disgust, I sold out, taking a loss of around $30,000, including commissions. Naturally my last

100 bales were sold at the lowest price of the reaction.

A few days later the market appealed to me again. I could not dismiss it from my mind, nor could I revise my original belief that it was in for a big move. So I re-bought my 20,000 bales. The same thing happened: up jumped the market on my buying order and, after that, right back down it came with a thud. Waiting irked me, so once more I sold my holdings, the last lot at the lowest price again.

This costly operation I repeated five times in six weeks, losing on each operation between $25,000 to $30,000. I became disgusted with myself. Here I had chipped away almost $200,000 with not even a semblance of satisfaction.

So I gave Harry Dache', my office manager, an order to have the Cotton ticker removed before my arrival the next morning. I did not want to be tempted to look at the Cotton market any more. It was too depressing, a mood not conducive to the clear thinking that is required at all times in the field of speculation.

And what happened?

Two days after I had the ticker removed and had lost all interest in Cotton, the market started up, and it never stopped until it had risen 500 points. In that remarkable rise it had but one reaction as great as "40" points.

I had thus lost one of the most attractive and soundest plays I had ever figured out. There were two basic reasons.

First, I lacked the patience to wait until the psychological time had arrived, pricewise, to begin my operation I had known that if Cotton ever sold up to 12 cents a pound it would be on its way to much higher prices. But no, I did not have the disciplined patience to wait. I thought I must make a few extra dollars quickly, before Cotton reached the buying point, and I acted before the market was ripe. Not only did I lose around $200,000 in actual money, but a profit of $1,000,000. For my original plan, well fixed in mind, contemplated the accumulation of 100,000 bales after the Pivotal Point had been passed. I could not have missed making a profit of 200 points or more on that move.

Secondly, to allow myself to become angry and disgusted with the Cotton market just because I had used bad judgment was not consistent with good speculative procedure. My loss was due wholly to lack of patience in awaiting the proper time to back up a preconceived opinion and plan.

I have long since learned, as all should learn, not to make excuses when wrong. Just admit it and try to profit by it. We all know when we are wrong. The market will tell the speculator when he is wrong, because he is losing money. When he first realizes he is wrong is the time to clear out, take his losses, try to keep smiling, study the record to determine the cause of his error, and await the next big opportunity. It is the net result over a period of time in which he is interested.

This sense of knowing when you are wrong even before the market tells you becomes, in time, rather highly developed. It is a subconscious tip-off. It is a signal from within that is based on knowledge of past market performances. Sometimes it is an advance agent of the trading formula. Let me explain more fully.

During the big Bull Market in the late twenties, there were times when I owned fairly large amounts of different stocks, which I held for a considerable period of time. During this period I never felt uneasy over my position whenever Natural Reactions occurred from time to time.

But sooner or later there would be a time when, after the market closed, I would become restive. That night I would find sound sleep difficult. Something would jog me into consciousness and I would awaken and begin thinking about the market Next morning I would be afraid, almost, to look at the newspapers. Something sinister would seem impending. But perhaps I would find everything rosy and my strange feelings apparently un-justified. The market might open higher. Its action could be perfect. It would be right at the peak of it's movement. One could almost laugh at his restless night. But I have learned to suppress such laughter.

For the next day the story would be strikingly different. No disastrous news, but simply one of those sudden market turning points after a prolonged movement in one direction. On that day I would be genuinely disturbed. I would be faced with the rapid liquidation of a large line. The day before, I could have liquidated my entire position within two points of the extreme movement. But today—what a vast difference.

I believe many operators have had similar experiences with that curious inner mind which frequently flashes the danger signal when everything marketwise is aglow with hope. It is just one of those peculiar quirks that develops from long study and association with the market.

Frankly, I am always suspicious of the inner mind tip-off and usually prefer to apply the cold scientific formula. But the fact remains that on many occasions I have benefited to a high degree by giving attention to a feeling of great uneasiness.

This curious sidelight on trading is interesting because the feeling of danger ahead seems to be pronounced only among those sensitive to market action, those whose thoughts have followed a scientific pattern in seeking to determine price movements. To the rank and file of persons who speculate the bullish or bearish feeling is simply based on something overheard or some published comment.

Bear in mind that of the millions who speculate in all markets only a few devote their entire time to speculation. With an overwhelming majority it is only a hit-and-miss affair, and a costly one. Even among intelligent business and professional men and retired men it is a sideline to which they give small attention. Most of them would not be trading in stocks if at some time a good tip had not been passed along by a broker or customers' man.

Now and then someone begins trading because he has a hot inside tip from a friend in the inner councils of a large corporation. Let me here relate a hypothetical case:

You meet your corporation friend at luncheon or at a dinner party. You talk general business for a time. Then you ask him about Great Shakes Corporation. Well, business is fine. It is just turning the corner and the future outlook is brilliant. Yes, the stock is attractive at this time. "A very good buy, indeed," he will say and perhaps in all sincerity. "Our earnings are going to be excellent, in fact better than for a number of years past. Of course you recall, Jim, what the stock sold for the last time we had a boom."

You are enthused and lose little time in acquiring shares.

Each statement shows better business than during the last quarter. Extra dividends are declared. The stock moves up and up. And you drift into pleasant paper profit dreams. But in the course of time the company's business begins slipping dreadfully. You are not appraised of the fact. You only know the price of the stock has tobogganed. You hasten to call your friend.

"Yes," he will say, "the stock has had quite a break. But it seems to be only temporary. Volume of business is down somewhat. Having learned the fact that the bears are attacking the stock. It's mostly short selling."

He may follow along with a lot of other platitudes, concealing the true reason. For he and his associates doubtless own a lot of the stock and have been selling as much and as rapidly as the market would take it since those first definite signs of a serious slump in their business appeared. To tell you the truth would simply invite your competition and perhaps the competition of your mutual friends in his selling campaign. It becomes almost a case of self-preservation.

So it is plain to see why your friend, the industrialist on the inside, can easily tell you when to buy. But he cannot and will not tell you when to sell. That would be equivalent almost to treason to his associates.

I urge you always to keep a little notebook with you. Jot down interesting market information: thoughts that may be helpful in the future; ideas that may be re-read from time to time; little personal observations you have made on price movements. On the first page of this little book I suggest you write—no, better yet print it in ink: "BEWARE OF INSIDE INFORMATION...ALL INSIDE INFORMATION!"

It cannot be said too often that in speculation and investment, success comes only to those who work for it. No one is going to hand you a lot of easy money. It is like the story of the penniless tramp. His hunger gave him the audacity to enter a restaurant and order "a big, luscious, thick, juicy steak," and, he added to the old waiter, "tell your boss to make it snappy." In a moment the waiter ambled back and whined: "De boss say if he had dat steak here he'd eat it himself." And if there was any easy money lying around, no one would be forcing it into your pocket.

## Chapter 7 - LIVERMORE SPEAKS

# THREE MILLION DOLLAR PROFIT

IN the preceding chapter, I related how by not exercising patience I missed being in on a play that would have netted a handsome profit. Now I shall describe an instance where I bided my time and the result of waiting for that perfect psychological moment.

In the summer of 1924, Wheat had reached a price that I term a Pivotal Point, so I stepped in with an initial buy order for five million bushels. At that time the Wheat market was an extremely large one, so that the execution of an order of this size had no appreciable effect on the price. Let me here indicate that a similar order given in a single stock would have been the equivalent of 50,000 shares.

Immediately after the execution of this order the market became dull for a few days, but it never declined below the Pivotal Point. The market then started up again and went a few cents higher than on the previous move; from which point it had a Natural Reaction and remained dull for a few days after which it resumed its advance.

As soon as it pierced the next Pivotal Point, I gave an order to buy another five million bushels. This was executed at an average price of 1½ cents above the Pivotal Point, which clearly indicated to me that the market was working itself into a strong position. Why? Because it was much more difficult to accumulate the second five million bushels than the first.

The ensuing day, instead of the market reacting as it had after the first order, it advanced 3 cents, which is exactly what it should have done if my analysis of the market was correct. From then on there developed what might be termed a real Bull Market. By that I mean an extensive movement had begun which I calculated would extend over a period of several months. I did not, however, fully realize the full possibilities that lay ahead.

Then, when I had 25 cents per bushel profit, I cashed in—and sat back and saw the market advance 20 cents more within a few days.

Right then I realized I had made a great mistake. Why had I been afraid of losing something I never really had?

I was altogether too anxious to convert a paper profit into actual cash, when I should have been patient and had the courage to play the deal out to the end. I knew that in due time, when the upward trend had reached its Pivotal Point, I would be given a danger signal in ample time.

I therefore decided to re-enter the market and went back at an average of 25 cents higher than that at which I had sold my first commitment. At first I had only the courage to make one commitment of five million bushels, which represented 50% of what I had originally sold out. However, from there on I stayed with the position until the danger signal gave warning.

On January 28, 1925, May Wheat sold at the high price of $2.05 per bushel. On February 11 it had reacted to $1.77.

During all this phenomenal advance in Wheat, there was another commodity, Rye, which had had an even more spectacular advance than Wheat.

However, the Rye market is a very small one compared to Wheat, so that the execution of a comparatively small order to buy would create a decidedly rapid advance.

During the above-described operations in rye, I frequently had a large personal commitment in the market, and there were others who had equally as large commitments. One other operator was reputed to have accumulated a line of several million bushels of futures, in addition to many millions of bushels of cash wheat, and in order to help his position in Wheat to have also accumulated large amounts of cash Rye. He was also reputed to have used the Rye market at times when Wheat began to waver by placing orders to buy Rye.

As stated, the Rye market being small and narrow in comparison to Wheat, the execution of any sizeable buying order immediately caused a rapid advance, and its reflection on Wheat prices was necessarily very marked. Whenever this method was used the public would rush in to buy Wheat, with the result that it sold into new high territory.

This procedure went on successfully until the major movement reached its end. During the time Wheat was having its reaction Rye reacted in a corresponding way, declining from its high price made on January 28, 1925, of $1.82 cents, to a price of $1.54, being a reaction of 28 cents against a reaction of 28 cents in Wheat.

On March 2, May Wheat had recovered to within 3 cents of its previous high, selling at $2.02, but Rye did not recover its decline in the same vigorous way as Wheat had, only being able to make a price of $1.70, which was 12 points below its previous high price.

Watching the market loosely, as I was at that time, I was struck forcibly by the fact that something was wrong, since, during all the big Bull Market, Rye had inevitably preceded the advance in Wheat.

Now, instead of becoming a leader of the Grain Pit in its advance, Rye was lagging. Wheat had already recovered most of its entire abnormal reaction, whereas Rye failed to do so by about 12 cents per bushel.

This action was something entirely new!

So I set to work analyzing, with a view to ascertaining the reason why Rye was not participating in the recovery proportionately to Wheat. The reason soon became evident. The public had a great interest in the Wheat market but none in Rye.

If this was a one-man, one major-speculator market, why, all of a sudden, was he neglecting it? I concluded that he either had no more interest in Rye and was out, or was so heavily involved in both markets that he was no longer in a position to make further commitments.

I decided then and there that it made no difference whether he was in or out of Rye—that eventually the result would be the same marketwise, so I put my theory to the test.

The last quotation on Rye was $1.69 bid, and having determined to find out the real position in Rye, I gave an order to sell 200,000 bushels "at the market." When I placed that order Wheat was quoted at $2.02. Before the order was executed Rye had sold off 3 cents per bushel, and two minutes after the order was filled it was back at $1.68.

I discovered by the execution of that order that there were not many orders under the market. However, I was not yet certain what might develop after, so I gave an order to sell another 200,000 bushels, with the same result—down it went 3 cents before the order was executed, but after the execution it only rallied 1 cent against the 2 cents previously.

I still entertained some doubt as to the correctness of my analysis of the position of the market, so I gave a third order to sell 200,000 bushels, with the same result—the market again went down, but this time there was no rally. It kept on going down on its own momentum.

That was the tip-off for which I was watching and waiting. If someone held a big position in the Wheat market and did not for some reason or other protect the Rye market (and what his reason was did not concern me), I felt confident that he would not, or could not, support the Wheat market.

So I immediately gave an order to sell my 5,000,000 bushels of May Wheat "at the market." It was sold from $2.01 to $1.99. That night it closed around $1.97 and Rye at $1.65. I was glad the last part of my order was completed below $2.00 because the $2.00 price was a Pivotal Point, and the market having broken through that Pivotal Point, I felt sure of my position. Naturally I never had any worries about that trade.

A few days later I bought my Rye in, which I had sold only as a testing operation to ascertain the position of the Wheat market, and chalked up a profit of $250,000 on the transaction.

In the meantime, I kept on selling Wheat until I had accumulated a short line of fifteen million bushels. March 16, May Wheat closed at $1.64 , and the next morning Liverpool was 3 cents lower than due, which on a parity basis should cause our market to open around $1.61.

Then I did something that experience taught me I should not do, namely, give an order at a specified price before the market opened. But temptation submerged my better judgment and I gave an order to buy five million bushels at $1.61, which was 3 cents below the previous night's close. The opening showed a price range of $1.61 to $1.54. Thereupon I said to myself: "It serves you right for breaking a rule you know you should not have broken."

But again it was a case of human instinct overcoming innate judgment. I would have bet anything that my order would be executed at the stipulated price of $1.61, which was the high of the opening price range.

Accordingly, when I saw the price of $1.54, I gave another order to buy five million bushels. Immediately thereafter I received a report: "Bought five million bushels May Wheat at $1.53."

Again I entered my order for another five million bushels. In less than one minute the report came; "Bought five million bushels at $1.53," which I naturally assumed was the price at which my third order had been filled. I then asked for a report on my first order. The following was handed to me:

"The first five million bushels reported to you filled your first order."

"The second five million bushels reported covered your second order.

"Here is the report on your third order:

     3,500,000 million bushels at 153

     1,000,000 bushels at 153 1/8

     500,000 bushels at 153 ¼"

The low price that day was $1.51 and next day Wheat was back to $1.64. That was the first time in my experience I had ever received an execution on a limited order of that nature. I had given an order to buy five million bushels at $1.61—the market opened at my bid price of $1.61 to 7 cents lower, $1.54, which represented a difference of $350,000.00.

A short time later I had occasion to be in Chicago, and asked the man who was in charge of placing my orders how it happened that I received such excellent execution of my first limited order.

He informed me that he happened to know there was an order in the market to sell thirty five million Bushels "at the market." That being the case, he realized that no matter how low the market might open there would be plenty of Wheat for sale at the lower opening price after the opening, so he merely waited until the opening range and then put in my order "at the market."

He stated that had it not been for my orders reaching the Pit as they did, the market would have had a tremendous break from the opening level.

The final net result of these transactions showed a profit of over $3,000,000.

This illustrates the value of having a short interest in speculative markets because the short interests become willing buyers when they cover their shorts, and those-willing buyers, the short sellers, act as a much-needed stabilizer in times of panic.

Today operations of this kind are not possible, as the Commodities Exchange Administration limits the size cf any one individual's position in the grain market to two million bushels, and while there has been no limit placed on the size of anyone's commitment in the stock market, it is equally impossible for any one operator to establish a sizeable short position under the existing rules in respect to selling short.

I therefore believe the day of the old speculator has gone. His place will be taken in the future by the semi-investor, who, while not able to make such large sums in the market quickly, will be able to make more money over a given period and be able to keep it. I hold the firm belief that the future successful semi-investor will only operate at the psychological time and will eventually realize a much larger percentage out of every minor or major movement than the purely speculative -minded operator ever did.

The future is bright for the intelligent, informed, patient, speculator.

NOTE: THIS IS THE END OF THE ACTUAL JESSE LIVERMORE TEXT FROM HIS ORIGINAL BOOK, EXCEPT FOR THE SECRET MARKET KEY WHICH IS IN THE REAR OF THE BOOK.

# Chapter 8

# JESSE LIVERMORE
## How To Trade In Stocks

Timing —*"Timing is everything"*

**$ TDT — Top Down Trading** —THE concept of "Top Down Trading" is very straightforward, before making any trade on any particular stock you must first check off the following items:

**$ TM —The Market** — Check the line of least resistance to establish the overall current market direction. Remember, Livermore never used the terms "Bull" or "Bear" because they forced a mind-set that he believed made the mind less flexible. He used the term *"Line of least resistance."* He checked to be sure the current line of least resistence was positive, negative or neutral—sideways. Be sure to check the exact market the stock trades in for instance: Dow, NASDAQ, or Amex—before executing the trade. It is essential to make sure the lines of least resistance are in the direction of your trade before entering the trade.

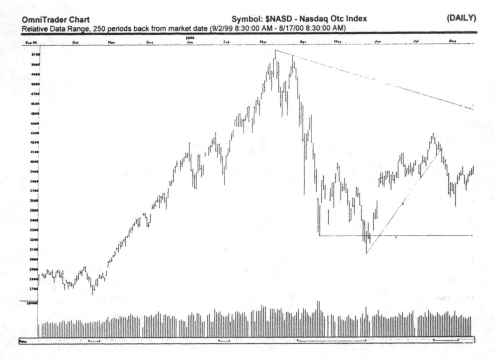

OmniTrader Chart                                  Symbol: $NASD - Nasdaq Otc Index                              (DAILY)
Relative Data Range, 250 periods back from market date (9/2/99 8:30:00 AM - 8/17/00 8:30:00 AM)

*The NASDAQ formed a Pivotal Point at the end of November and the
"line of least resistance" was clearly upward until March when it formed
a Pivotal Point and changed its momentum and the "line of least resistance became negative" and started downward.*

**$ TIG — THE INDUSTRY GROUP** — Check the specific industry
group if you are considering a trade in ATT check out the Telecommunication Long Distance Group. If you are looking at a trade in
Haliburton, check out the Oil Well Drilling group. If you are looking at
a trade in Harrah Entertainment check out the Gambling Group, make
sure the group is moving in the correct direction, the line of least resistance to provide a profit for you on the trade you have selected. In the
example on the following page the trade is in the Internet Industry Group.

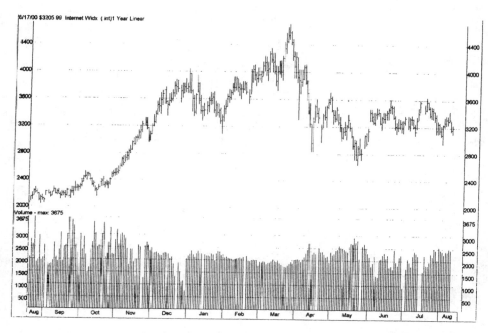

6/17/00 $3205 99 Internet Widx ( int)1 Year Linear

*The Internet Industry Group began its ascent at the end of October, the same time as the NASDAQ and was a leading group at the time. It topped out simultaneously with the overall NASDAQ index in March/ April and gave a clear sign that the line of least resistance was rolling over to the downside. The Internet Industry Group therefore confirmed the action of the NASDAQ.*

$ TT — TANDEM TRADING — Check the stock and the Sister Stock and compare them. If you are going to trade in General Motors check a Sister Stock like Ford or Chrysler. If you are going to trade Best Buy than check out Circuit City–a Sister Stock. Tandem Trading requires the trader to place two stocks of the same group next to each other. The stocks chosen for this example are Yahoo (yhoo) and America Online (aol).

*(see chart on following page)*

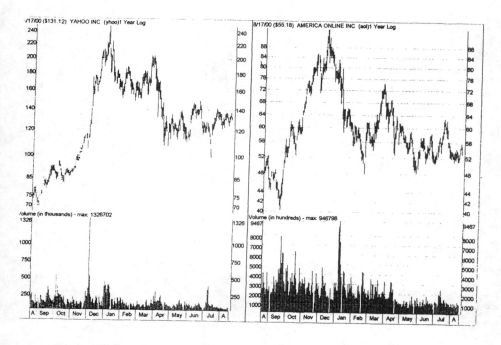

*Both Yahoo and AOL topped out together in December giving a clear signal that the line of least resistence for this industry group was negative. Because this was a leading group it also acted as a precursor of what was to come in March/April, when the market went into a steep decline.*

**$ TDT — TOP TRADING DOWN** — The final step in Top Down Trading is to examine all four factors at the same time—The Market, The Industry Group and the Tandem Stocks and the actual stock in one glance. The example is the Internet Industry group as seen on the following page.

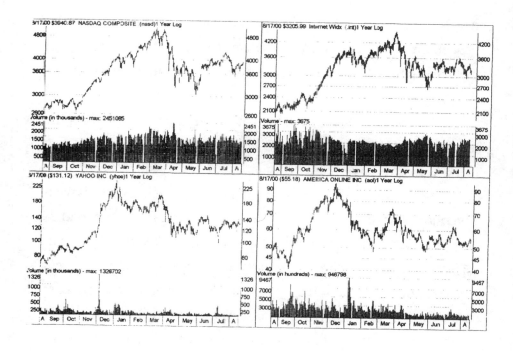

*In this example, the Tandem Stocks clearly indicated first that they had topped, and the line of least resistance was down in December. The Industry group followed in March/ April along with the overall NASDAQ as it rolled over and descended.*

Due Diligence—do a final thorough analysis of the individual stock you have decided to trade. This is your responsibility, your obligatory "Due Diligence." This final step would be similar to traveling down the runway–but not lift off— a final chance to change your mind before you "pull the trigger" and buy the stock. This final step must be completed by you, and you alone...make this decision on your own—it's your money.

An ex-military friend of mine compares this approach of Livermore's to the steps the U.S. Marines follow before they assault a beach. They study all the factors on all the possible beaches; they analyze all these factors as carefully as they can with the full knowledge that the assault will not be perfect, no matter what the analysis reveals to them.

There will always be unknown factors, the main one being the unpredictable human factor in assaulting a beach or playing the stock market...there is always the "Human Factor" to consider.

What the Marines are doing in planning beach assaults is what Livermore was trying to do, weigh all the factors until the preponderance of evidence has been assembled, and all the odds were in his favor. It isn't easy: you must not be too early, too late, too timid, too aggressive and you can't commit all your troops at one time, but you must strike when the final moment presents itself as overwhelming evidence. In other words, you must use your own judgment to achieve control of your financial destiny. The Livermore Laws:

*Wait until the Preponderance of Evidence is in your Favor.*
*Use Top Down Trading.*
*Be patient!*
—Jesse Livermore

*"UNDERSTANDING INDUSTRY GROUP ACTION*
*IS ESSENTIAL TO SUCCESSFUL TRADING"*
—Jesse Livermore

## Industry Group Action

Livermore loved to fish. His winters in Palm Beach were more than a vacation. It took him away from New York and the market, even though he often played the market from E.F. Hutton's Palm Beach office.

The Atlantic Ocean fascinated him. It made him feel small. His life fell into better focus when he got out onto the ocean. Some of his greatest thinking was done fishing, trolling along the hundred fathom bar a few miles off Palm Beach, down to Key West, following the great underwater canyon that ran from Cuba to Nova Scotia, a nautical highway for the great gypsy fish, the pelagic predators.

He enjoyed solitary thinking on the back deck while cruising easily on his 300 foot yacht the "Anita Venetian," as he headed down to Key West for some tarpon fishing, using guides, and watching those great Florida Keys sunsets. To him, the ocean was always exciting, ever-changing, and it refreshed his soul and cleared his mind for deeper thoughts. He believed this time on the sea led him to important discoveries like: The importance of Industry Group action.

In the 1920's Livermore made another important discovery that he applied to his trading strategy: *"INDUSTRY GROUP MOVEMENTS."* Livermore deduced from observation that stocks did not move alone, when they moved. They moved in Industry Groups. If U. S. Steel rose then sooner or later Bethlehem, Republic, and Crucible would follow along. Livermore observed this time and time again, and it became an important trading tool in his arsenal.

Livermore: "The most intelligent way to get one's mind attuned to market conditions and to be successful is to make a deep study of Industry Groups in order to distinguish the good groups from the bad: get long of those which are in a promising position and get out of those Industry Groups which are not.

"It has been shown time and time again that on Wall Street

people very often fail to see the thing that is right in front of them. We now have millions of people interested in the security markets, where there were only thousands in former years. I cannot emphasize too strongly the importance of the utmost discrimination in the purchase of securities by first examining Industry Groups.

"Stay away from weak groups!

"Just as I would avoid the weak stocks in the weak industries, I would favor the strongest stocks in the strongest industries. The trader must, of course, be willing and able to revise any forecasts and positions in the light of developments that come to hand from day-to-day and move quickly, if factors have moved against the trader."

## WHY DO INDUSTRY GROUPS MOVE TOGETHER

The *GROUP MOVEMENT premise* was quite simple to Livermore. He explained:

"If the basic reasons are sound why U.S. Steel's business should come into favor in the stock market, then the rest of the steel group should also follow for the same basic reasons. This, of course also works for the short side of the market—when a group goes out-of-favor for basic reasons it will include *ALL THE STOCKS* in that industry group."

It was also an important clue for Livermore if a particular stock in the favored group, did not move up and prosper with the others, this could mean that perhaps this particular stock was weak or sick, and therefore might be a good short sale or at the very least, a trader should be cautious in buying any stock that does not follow the overall group action.

The only exception to "Group Movement" is where a single stock may make up over fifty percent or more of the total sales of the group—sooner or later the rest of the group must follow this stock.

7-15-99         LUCENT TECHNOLOGIES INC (LU)       77.62

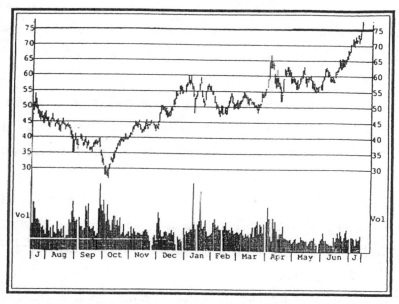

7-15-99 TELECOMMUNICATIONS/EQIPMENT-SERVICE WIDX   186.78

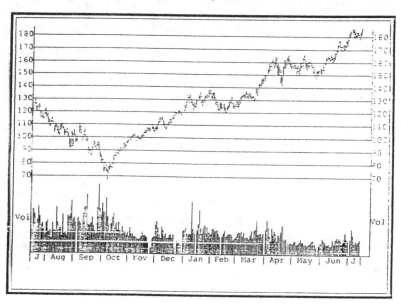

*Note Example: These charts clearly reflect how important the "DOMI-NANT" stock is to the group...in fact you could say in cases, such as this example, the leading stock "IS" the group.*

**$** **FCL — F**OLLOWING THE **C**URRENT **L**EADERS **—** Livermore developed a sophisticated system of *"FOLLOWING THE CURRENT LEADERS."* His interest in the leaders was two fold:

He said, "Confine your studies of stock market movements to the prominent issues of the day, the leaders. It is where the action is—if you cannot make money out of the leading active issues, you are not going to make money out of the stock market.

"Second, this will also keep your trading universe small and controllable, so you can focus and trade the stocks with the greatest potential. Don't let greed drive your moves by trying to catch the exact top and the exact bottom."

Livermore also believed that timing should never be dictated by high prices. High prices were never a timing signal to sell a stock. Livermore said: "Just because a stock is selling at a high price does not mean it won't go higher." Livermore was also just as comfortable on the short side, if that was the direction of the trend. "Just because a stock has fallen in price does not mean that it won't go lower. I never buy a stock on declines, and I never short a stock on rallies."

Buying stocks as they made new highs and selling short as they made new lows was a contrarian point of view in his day. Livermore let the market tell him what to do. He got his clues and his cues...from what the market told him. He did not anticipate, he followed the message he received from the tape. And some stocks keep making new high or lows, for a very long time, and can be held for a very long time.

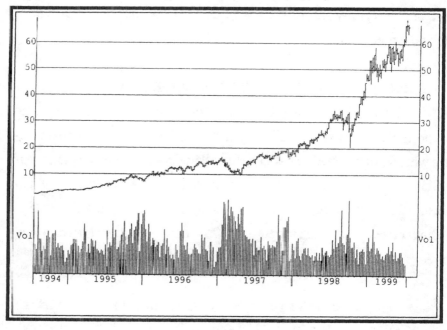

7-15-99        CISCO SYSTEMS INC (CSCO)        66.56

*Note Example: Cisco Systems, a leader in networking solutions for the Internet, has basically gone up for five straight years. A 1000 share position in 1994 would have cost $2,000; that investment, five years later, in 1999, would be worth $70,000.*

Livermore: "I also believe in trading the market leader, go with the most powerful stock in the group-don't look for the bargain, the weak sister, go with the leader, the anchor, the strongest stock in the group. Also note that this may not always be the conventional leader of the group. Occasionally, a smaller, well-managed stock in the group will assume leadership, perhaps with a new product, and knock out the old leader. Keep alert! Choose the most powerful stock in the group, not the best bargain or a beaten down stock poised to recover.

Livermore observed that these groups went in and out of favor with each new major bull market. The leading stock groups of one major market move most likely would "NOT" be the leading groups of the next major market.

## CALLING THE TOPS USING INDUSTRY GROUPS

It was Livermore's experience that stock-group-behavior is an important key to overall market direction, a key ignored by most traders whether they were big traders or small traders. He believed the groups often provided the key to changes in trends. As favored groups got weaker and collapsed it usually meant a correction in the market. This is how he called the market turn in 1907, and 1929, the leaders rolled over first.

**$ TT — "TANDEM TRADING" — LIVERMORE INVENTS — "SISTER STOCK TRADING METHOD"** — "Tandem Trading" or "Sister Stock" trading, as Livermore used to say to his sons, Jesse Jr. and Paul, is essential to the successful investor. "Boys, never look at only one stock—look at two—track two. Why? Because stocks in the same group always move together. TRACKING TWO STOCKS adds a great confirming psychological dimension to your mental abilities, when you can visualize that they move in tandem and that they confirm the movements of each other. It is twice as hard "NOT" to follow the correct signal when you see with your own eyes that the Sister Stocks actually move in tandem and therefore give you absolute confirmation.

It was Tandem Trading that allowed Livermore to properly police his investments. Once the investment was made Livermore heightened his "vigilance" and continued "due diligence" by everyday observation of not just the stock he had purchased—he always maintained his daily Tandem Trading or Sister Stock observations looking for clues to what was happening and what was about to happen.

For Livermore the evidence, the clues, the truth, was always in the market itself and visible if a person knew how to read the evidence, the way a forensic investigator examines the details of a crime scene—clues become obvious to him that are visible to no one else. All a person needs to do is observe what the market is telling him and evaluate it. The answer lies in the market facts—the challenge is to properly interpret the facts that are being presented. He told his sons: "It's like being a great detective working on a great case that never ends—you never know it all!"

Tandem Trading, the use of Sister Stocks, was one of the great secrets of Livermore's trading techniques and remains just as valid today as it did in years gone by.

This technique is an essential element in both "Top Down Trading" and in the maintenance of the trade after it has been completed.

"SUCCESSFUL TRADERS ALWAYS FOLLOW THE LINE OF LEAST RESISTANCE—FOLLOW THE TREND—THE TREND IS YOUR FRIEND"—Livermore

The examples on the following page illustrate the use of "Tandem Trading" or "Sister Stock" trading.

7-15-99    GENERAL MOTORS CORPORATION (GM)    68.06

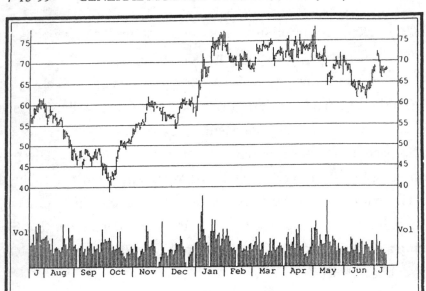

7-15-99    FORD MOTORS CO DEL (F)    68.06

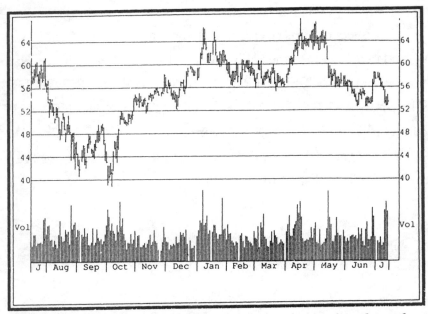

*Note Example: The charts above illustrate that nothing has changed from Livermore's day—the automotive group moves in unison. General Motors and Ford basically move in lock-step.*

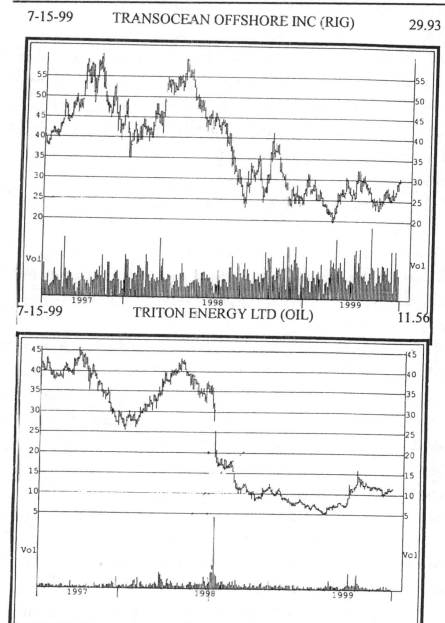

Note Example: *The charts illustrated above are a reflection of part of the "oil patch group." As the price of oil plummeted in the late spring of 1998, Transocean and Triton Energy, both off-shore oil drillers, were hit hard because their profit margins were threatened. All the drillers joined hands and took a deep dive in the price of their stocks.*

**§** **RPP — REVERSAL PIVOTAL POINTS** — The Pivotal Point theory allowed Livermore the chance to buy at the exact "right time." Pivotal Points were defined by Livermore as: —the perfect psychological moment to make a trade. Reversal Pivotal Points mark a change in trend. He never wanted to buy at the lowest price or sell at the top. He wanted to buy at the right time, and sell at the right time.

This required him to have patience and wait for the perfect Pivotal Point trading situation to develop. If the right conditions did not all coincide on a particular stock he was following, he didn't care, because he knew that the proper pattern would appear sooner or later on another stock. Patience...patience...patience—that was his key to timing success.

Livermore always considered "TIME" as a real and essential trading element. He would often times say: "It's not the thinkin' that makes the money—it's the sittin' and waitin' that makes the money."

This has been often incorrectly interpreted by many people to mean Livermore would buy a stock, and then sit and wait for it to move. This is not so. There were many occasions where Livermore sat and waited in cash, until the right situation appeared. Much of his success was in his ability to sit and wait patiently in cash until the "perfect situation presented itself to him." When these conditions came together, when as many of the odds as possible were in his favor, then and only then, like a cobra, he would strike.

Buying on the Pivotal Point assured him the best chance of coming into the situation:

**"JUST AS THE ACTION WAS ABOUT TO BEGIN."**

And once he was sure of his play, he wasn't afraid to make his commitment. He wasn't called the "Boy Plunger" for nothing.

Livermore: "When a speculator can determine the Pivotal Point of a stock and interpret the action at that point, he may make a commitment with the positive assurance of being right from the start.

"But bear in mind when using Pivotal Points in anticipating movements, that if the stock does not perform as it should, after crossing the Pivotal Point, this is an important danger signal which must be heeded immediately. Every time I lost patience and failed to await the Pivotal Points and fiddled around for some easy profits. I would lose money.

"I have found the study of Pivotal Points fascinating almost beyond belief. You will find a golden field for personal research. You will derive a singular pleasure and satisfaction from successful trades based on your own judgment. You will discover that profits made in this way are immensely more gratifying than any which could possibly come from tips, or the guidance of someone else. If you make your own discovery, trade your own way, exercise patience, and watch for the danger signals, you will develop a proper trend of thinking.

"This Pivotal Points theory applies to trading in commodities just as it does to trading in stocks. I never considered this method of trading Pivotal Points as a foolproof perfect method of picking winners, but it represents an "Essential" part of my trading strategy.

"I have stated on a few occasions that there will be a lot more to perfecting the use of Pivotal Points in the future. I am sure people will develop better trading methods from this basic premise. I promise that I will not be jealous of their success.

"It's okay to mentally anticipate the action of the market, or a stock, but take no action until the market has confirmed that you are correct, by its action: DON'T ANTICIPATE MARKET MOVES WITH YOUR HARD EARNED CASH.

"It's okay to mentally speculate on future moves, but wait until you get a confirming signal from the market that your judgment is correct, then—and only then, you can move with your money. Pivotal Points are essential, as a confirming signal, but you must let them play out.

"Often, the market will go contrary to what a speculator has predicted. At these times the successful speculator must abandon his predictions, and follow the action of the market. A prudent speculator never argues with the tape, remember: MARKETS ARE NEVER WRONG—OPINIONS OFTEN ARE.

"Timing is everything to a speculator. It is never "if" a stock was going to move. It is "when" a stock is going to move and in which direction—up, down or sideways."

"The crash of '29 brought about my complete belief in Pivotal Points. Black Tuesday was the biggest Pivotal Point in the history of the stock market, the market fell 11.7% in one single day and kept right on going down.

"I cannot over emphasize that Pivotal Points, once I understood them, became one of my true trading keys, a trading technique that was basically unknown in a formal way in stock speculation in the twenties and early thirties. Pivotal Points are a TIMING device. I use them to get in and out of the market.

"Once again, the Reversal Pivotal Point is not easily defined. In my mind it is:

*"A CHANGE IN BASIC MARKET DIRECTION—THE PERFECT PSYCHOLOGICAL TIME AT THE BEGINNING OF A NEW MOVE, IT IS A MAJOR CHANGE IN THE BASIC TREND.*

"For my style of trading it did not matter if it was at the bottom or the top of a long term trending move, because I would buy or sell any stock, long or short.

"The *'Reversal Pivotal Point,'* flags for me optimum trading timing."

7-15-99          SCHLUMBERGER LTD (SLB)          64.56

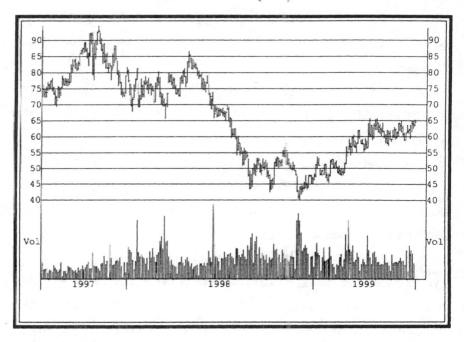

*Note Example: SCHLUMBERGER, an oil drilling and service company, made two clear Reversal Pivotal Points-the first in late 1997 that led to a decline in price and a second Reversal Pivotal Point at the end of 1998 that led to an increase in price.*

"Reversal Pivot points are almost always accompanied by a heavy increase in *volume*, a climax of buying, which is met with a barrage of selling—or vice-versa. Increased *Volume* is an essential element in understanding Pivotal Points—it must be present to confirm the Pivotal Point. This battle, this war, between buyers and sellers causes the stock to reverse its direction, top out, or bottom out in a decline. It is the start of a new direction in trend for the stock. These important confirming *volume* spurts often end the day with a 50 percent to 500 percent increase in the average daily volume of the stock.

"Reversal Pivotal Points usually came after long-term trending moves. This is one of the reasons why I always felt patience was so necessary for success in catching the big moves. You need patience to be sure that you have identified a true Reversal Pivotal Point of a stock. I developed tests.

"First of all I would send out a *"probe."* I would buy a small percentage of the stock position that I would eventually establish, if I was correct with the first trade.

"I had one final test I used to confirm if a Reversal Pivot Point had occurred. I looked at the industry group, and at least one other stock in the group, to see if it had the same pattern. This was the final confirmation I needed to point out that I was on the right track.

**$ CPP — E**VALUATING **C**ONTINUATION **P**IVOTAL **P**OINTS **—** "It is essential to understand that the *"Reversal Pivotal Point"* marks a definite change in direction. The *"Continuation Pivotal Points"* confirm the move is proceeding in the proper direction.

"Beyond the Reversal Pivotal Point there is a second very important type of Pivotal Point I call the *'Continuation Pivotal Point.'* This usually occurs during a trending move as a natural reaction for a stock in a definite trend. This is a potential additional entry point in an ongoing move, or a chance to increase your position, providing the stock emerges from the Continuation Pivot Point, headed in the same direction as it was before the correction. I define a Continuation Pivotal Point as a consolidation where the stock pauses in its ascent, as a general sometimes pauses in a major assault to let his supply lines catch up to his troops and provide his men with a rest. It is usually a natural reaction of the stock. The prudent speculator, however, will carefully observe which way the stock will emerge from this consolidation, and not anticipate."

7-15-99          SCHLUMBERGER LTD (SLB)          64.56

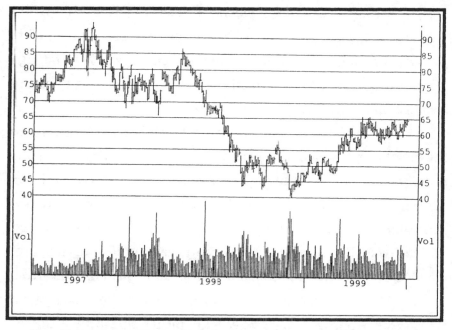

*Note Example: SCHLUMBERGER formed a Continuation Pivotal Point in mid-1998 when it hit $86 confirming the descent, in this case to—$40–near the end of 1998.*

"For me, a stock's price is never too high to buy, or too low to sell-short. By waiting for these Continuation Pivotal Points signals, it gave me the opportunity to either open a new position or to add to a current position, if I had already established one. Do not chase a stock if it gets away from you—let it go. I would rather wait and pay more, after the stock had regrouped and formed a new Continuation Pivotal Point, because this Continuation Pivotal Point provides a confirmation and insurance that the stock will most likely continue with its move. It gives a stock a chance to take a breath and consolidate often allowing the stock's ratio of earnings and sales to catch up to the price of the stock.

"Conversely, this Pivotal Point theory can also be used to find successful short -selling plays. I looked for stocks that traded down to a new low for the last year or so. If they formed a "False Pivotal Point" that is: if they rallied from this new low and then dropped down through the new low, they were most likely to continue down from there and establish additional new lows for the move.

"By correctly catching the Pivotal Points it enabled me to make my initial purchase at the right point so that I had an entry point at the right price from the beginning of the move. This insured that I was never in a loss position, and I could therefore ride out the normal stock fluctuations without risking my own capital. Once the stock had moved off the Pivotal Point I was only risking my 'paper profits' not my 'precious capital,' because I was 'in profit' from the beginning of the trade.

"My early years of getting crushed because I had bought the stock at the wrong time in its move, gave me the clue to my theory of using Pivotal Points. On many of those trades I was *never in profit.* If you buy before the Pivotal Point is established then you may be early. This is dangerous because the stock may never form a proper Pivotal Point to clearly establish its direction. But you must be careful—if you buy more than 5% or 10% above the initial Pivotal Point, then you may be late. You may have lost your edge because the move is already well under way.

"The 'Pivotal Point' gives the only tip-off you need to trade and win. A speculator has to be patient, because it takes time for a stock to run out its logical and natural course and form a proper Pivotal Point. It will not be willed or forced forward by an impatient trader. It will come as a natural event.

"The key to my later theory of trading is to trade: ONLY ON THE PIVOTAL POINTS. I have always made money when I was patient and traded on the Pivotal Points.

"I also believe that often the largest part of a stock movement occurs in the last two weeks or so of the play. I call it the—Final Markup Phase—the same thing applies for commodities. So, once again, a speculator must be patient, get into position and wait, but at the same time a trader must be completely alert for the clues when they come, good or bad and then take action to either buy or sell his position."

$ S — Spikes — ODR — One Day Reversals — I was very wary of price *"Spikes"* accompanied by abnormally heavy volume of at least a fifty-percent increase versus the average. This often led to *"One Day Reversals."*

"I always looked for aberrations in the market. An aberration to me was any strong deviation from what was normal for the stock. I considered a spike in the stock price, high volume, and low volume, all aberrations, deviations from the norm, a straying from what would be considered normal for the stock. To me these were possible danger signals, and often a signal to exit a trade.

"A strong signal for me, a signal that made me sit up and take notice was the *"ONE DAY REVERSAL."* This is a stock movement that often happens at the end of a long-term move.     I define it as: *'A One Day Reversal occurs where the high of the day is higher than the high of the previous day, but the close of the day is below the close of the previous day, and the volume of the current day is higher than the volume of the previous day.'"*

7-15-99          SCHWAB CHARLES CORP NEW (SCH)          55.37

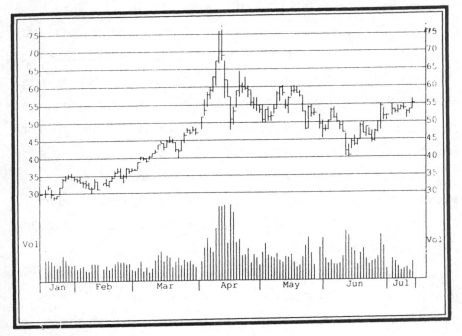

*Note Example:-In this case Charles Schwab, a brokerage firm, had a dramatic rise of over 15 points in 3 days that developed into a spike. During the last day of the ascent the rally breaks down near the end of the day and the price of the stock falls and closes near the low of the day. The next morning it opens and falls further. These one-day reversals are often accompanied by increased volume.*

This scenario was a screaming "danger signal" to Livermore. Why? Because all during its rise, following the trend, the line of least resistance, it had only normal reactions. Then all of a sudden it had an abnormal, sudden aberrant reaction...it moved 15 points in only 3 days on heavy volume, it has broken its pattern. This is a danger signal and MUST BE HEEDED!

It was Livermore's position that if you had the "PATIENCE" to sit with the stock all during its rise, now after the "ONE DAY REVERSAL" you must have the "COURAGE" to do the right thing and acknowledge this danger signal. You must now consider selling the stock. Livermore believed in "PATIENCE" and "COURAGE."

$ BONH — BREAKOUTS ON A NEW HIGH — "NEW HIGHS" were always good news for Jesse Livermore. To him it meant that the stock had pushed through the overhead resistance and was very likely to advance. Livermore was not a chartist. He calculated everything from a numerical base.

Below are several "New High Breakout Formations" that appeared on a regular basis to Livermore in numerical form. Charts have been used for expediency.

7-15-99                    BEST BUY INC (BBY)                    76 18

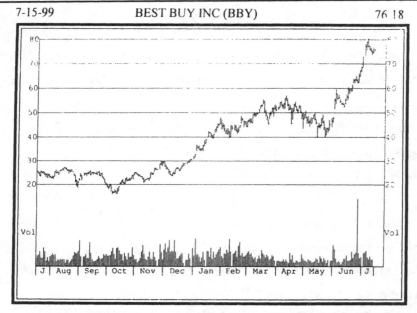

*Note example: Best Buy, a consumer retailer of electronics, appliances, and entertainment software, broke out of a long consolidation at $30 in December of 1998 and kept right on climbing to new highs.*

7-15-99          NORTHERN TELECOM LTD (NT)          94.06

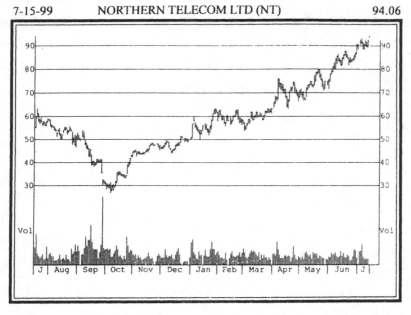

*Note Example: Nortel Networks, a manufacturer of telecommunication equipment, formed a strong Reversal Pivotal Point at–$30–in September of 1998 and powered through to a new all-time high of $65 in April of 1999.*

**$ BOCB — Breakout from a Consolidating Base** — Stocks sometimes take time to consolidate and build a base before continuing their movement. This base allows the stock a breather and a chance for the sales and earnings to catch up to the new valuation of the stock. In many ways it is similar to a Continuation Pivotal Point in function, although the formation looks different, and the time period is usually longer for the Consolidating Base to form. When the Consolidating Base occurs the same patience must be applied to the situation as required with the Continuation Pivot Point—*"don't anticipate"* wait for the stock to tell you by its action which direction it is going to go. Below are some examples of a Consolidating Base.

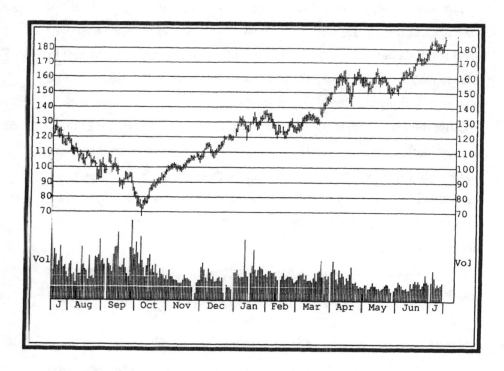

*Note Example: From early January until late March, a consolidating base was formed. A breakout occured.*

From the beginning of his trading Livermore was keenly aware of volume. It was obvious to him that as the volume drastically changed it was a clear "Aberration" or a "Deviation" that is, a change from the normal. The question was it— *"Accumulation"* or was it— *"Distribution."* And Livermore was an expert at detecting *"DISTRIBUTION."* He had formed a strong opinion on that subject, because he knew how stocks were distributed by the "pool runners" of his day. The "pool runners" were charged with distributing the stock of the insiders who had formed a pool with their own stock and given the job of selling, distributing the stock, to an expert like Livermore.

Stocks were never distributed on the way up...they were distributed on the way down. The reasoning was simple—people will not take losses, the public will hold on to their stock as it drops and wait until it rallies back to the price where they bought it so they can sell it. This is why so many stocks falter as they rally back to the old high. The people who bought at the high are now selling to get their money back— because they were scared—they got a fright—and are happy to get there money back. This is one of the reasons why Livermore bought stocks on new-high-breakouts. Simply stated, with a new high breakout, there was most likely no stock overhanging the market, waiting to be sold on the uptick, it was usually clear open air above the old high, once the stock broke out into clear skies.

A change in volume is an *"alert signal."* It almost always means that there is something afoot, a change, a difference, and an aberration. It therefore always caught Livermore's attention. Was it the volume leading to the "blow off" setting the stage for a decline or was it "real interest" in the stock, ready to drive it higher. Livermore never searched for the reason "why." He simply took it as a truism that volume was an alert signal. It was "happening" that was "why" enough for him. The reasons would be revealed later when the chance to make money was gone. Don't try and figure out why something is happening. Let the market give you the clues, the movement of the stock is empirical evidence, wait for a later day to figure out the motive.

Conversely, if there is heavy volume, but the prices stall and do not go up and make new highs and there is no strong continuation of the current move—beware—this is often a strong clue, a warning that the stock may have topped out.

*Note: At the end of a market move heavy volume is usually pure distribution, as stocks go from strong hands into weak hands, from the professionals to the public. It is deceptive to the public who view this heavy volume as the mark of a vibrant, healthy market going through a normal correction, not a top or a bottom.*

## SUMMARY

Livermore was always alert to look toward volume indications as a key signal at the end of a major move, either in the entire market or an individual stock. Also he observed that at the end of a long move, it was not uncommon for stocks to suddenly spike up in a straight shot with heavy volume and then stop, and roll at the top, exhausted, and then retreat, downward—never to make a "new high" before the onslaught of a major correction.

This last gasp of heavy volume also provided a great opportunity to sell out any illiquid large holdings. He knew it was foolish to ever try to catch the tops or the bottoms of the moves. It is always better to sell large holdings into an advancing strong market when there is plenty of volume. The same is true on the short side, you are best to cover the short position after a steep fast decline. Livermore never tried to catch tops or bottoms.

7-15-99       CAPITAL ONE FINANCIAL CORP (COF)       48.93

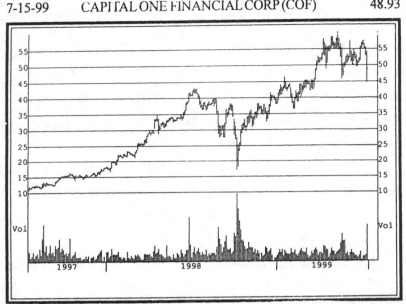

*Note Example: Capital One Financial's terrific volume, and spike down, in early October shows a clear "high-volume-climax-bottom" that indicates the downward trend has ended. Be alert that VOLUME is often a key confirming signal to indicate a change in direction.*

## LINE OF LEAST RESISTANCE

The most important thing in Livermore's mind for the successful speculator was to determine the direction of the "LINE OF LEAST RESISTANCE" for the market, for the industry group, and finally for the stock. Put the wind at your back, and sail forward easily, keep the wind out of your face, and when the market hits the doldrums getting nowhere, moving sideways, then get out, take a break, have some fun, go fishing. Come back into the market when the wind has picked up again, and the sailing is clear and good. Staying out of the action is always difficult for an active trader, but Livermore grew to know it was essential at times to be out of the market, sitting, waiting in cash.

*"There is nothing more important than your emotional balance."*          *—Livermore*

## STOCKS HAVE PERSONALITIES

Livermore: "Every stock is like a human being: it has a personality—a distinctive personality—aggressive, reserved, hyper, highstrung, volatile, boring, direct, logical, predictable, unpredictable. I often study stocks like I would study people, after a while their reactions to certain circumstance become more predicable.

"I am not the first to observe this. I know people who have made a lot of money in the stock market by analyzing the personality of a stock, and following that personality, reacting to it by buying and selling it according to its personality traits. And beware, not often, but sometimes, personalities change.

"I firmly believe that as long as a stock is acting properly—progressing, with normal reactions such as consolidations, corrections, and proceeding in the direction of the trend there is nothing to fear, no reason for a speculator to concern himself. And the fact that a stock is selling in new high territory should only encourage the speculator.

"On the other hand a speculator must never become complacent, or relaxed to the point that he misses the clues that the stock has topped out, and is creating a Pivotal Point that will set it off in a new direction, perhaps a reversal in trend. My motto: 'Be ever vigilant for the danger signs.'"

## KNOWLEDGE AND PATIENCE

"The essentials to stock market success are knowledge and patience. Few people succeed in the market because they have no patience. They have a strong desire to get rich quickly. They buy mostly when a stock is going up and is near the top. They are not willing to buy when the stock goes down and wait until it forms a pivotal point and begins to recover—if it does recover.

"In the long run, patience counts more than any other single element except knowledge. The two really go hand in hand. Those who want to succeed through their investments should learn that simple truth. You must also investigate before you buy and then you are sure your position is a sound one.

"Never let yourself become discouraged by the fact that your securities are moving slowly. Good securities in time appreciate sufficiently to make it well worthwhile to have had patience.

"The only time to buy is when you know they will go up. When you have as many factors in your favor as possible. These situations come along only rarely—the trader must wait, be patient, sooner or later the right situation will come along.

"I traded to beat the game and a big part was having the right timing. My quest was never ending: To refine and develop the Pivotal Point approach, my approach to trading new highs, finding the industry leaders and the best industry group. These theories were all developed after much experience and effort. But it was the mental challenge that was always my passion and challenge.

"But like anyone else, I also enjoyed what the money could do. Having money was a good experience."

## Chapter 9

# JESSE LIVERMORE
# How To Trade in Stocks

**$ MM — MONEY MANAGEMENT —** Money Management was one of the three pieces of the puzzle that fascinated Livermore: Timing, Money Management, and Emotional Control.

Livermore had five main rules in managing his money. He attempted over the years to explain his entire trading theory to his sons—Money Management was a big part of it.

One day he called his two sons into the library at "Evermore." He sat behind the massive desk, the two boys sat down in front of him. He leaned forward and took a wad of cash out of his pocket. He peeled off ten one dollar bills. He did this twice, then folded the bills and handed each boy a pack of ten ones.

The boys sat looking at him each holding their money. "Boys, always carry your money folded and in your left pocket. Go ahead do it. You can keep the money."

The boys did as they were told and put the folded money in their left pockets. "You see pickpockets always go for a person's wallet, usually in their back pocket. Or they will come up behind you and go for your right front pocket, because most people are right handed. You all right with this so far, boys?" He asked.

The boys nodded.

He continued. "Alright, that's why you keep your paper money folded in your left pocket. See, if a pickpocket gets into your left pocket, and he gets that close to your balls, you're going to know about it."

The boys looked at each other.

Their father continued. "Don't ever lose your cash boys—that's the moral of this story. Keep it close to your balls, and don't let anyone near it."

## Livermore Money Management Rule Number One:

"I like to call this my probe system. Don't lose money—don't lose your stake, don't lose your line. A speculator without cash is like a store-owner with no inventory. Cash is your inventory, your lifeline, your best friend—without cash you're out of business. Don't lose your damn line!

"It is wrong and dangerous to establish your full stock position at only one price. Rather, you must first decide how many shares you want to trade. For example, if you want to purchase 1000 shares as the full final position do it like this:

"Start with a 200 share purchase on the pivot point—if the price goes up then buy an additional 200 shares, still within the pivot point range. If it keeps rising, buy another 200 shares. Then see how it reacts, if it keeps on rising or corrects and then rises you can go ahead and purchase the final 400 shares.

"It is very important to note that each additional purchase must be at a higher price. The same rules, of course, would apply to selling short, only each short sale would be at a lower price than the preceding sale.

"The basic logic is simple and concise: each trade, as it is established toward the total 1000 share position, must always show the speculator a profit on his prior trades. The fact that each trade showed a profit is living proof, hard evidence, that your basic judgment is correct in the trade. *The stock is going in the right direction*—and that is all the proof you need, and conversely if you lose money...you know immediately that your judgment was wrong.

"The tough part for the inexperienced speculator is to pay more for each position. Why? Because everyone wants a bargain. It goes against human nature to pay more for each trade. People want to buy at the bottom and sell at the top. The psychological wrestle is not to fight the facts, not to hope, not to argue with the tape, for the tape is always correct—there is no place in speculating for hoping, for guessing, for fear, for greed...for emotions. The tape tells the truth, but often there is a lie buried in the human interpretation.

"Finally, the speculator may choose a different ratio for purchasing the stock. The trader could, for instance, purchase thirty percent as the first probe position, thirty as the second and forty for the final purchase.

"It is up to each individual speculator to decide the ratio that works best for him. I have simply outlined here what works best for me. The main rule is comprised of three factors first: do not take your entire position all at once.

"The second factor is: wait for confirmation of your judgment— PAY MORE FOR EACH LOT YOU BUY.

"And the third factor is to: establish in your mind the total amount of shares you want to purchase, or specify the amount of dollars you are willing to commit, before you begin the trade."

# MONEY MANAGEMENT
## PROBES

EXPLANATION:
First determine the amount of shares you want to acquire, or use dollar amount. Then acquire your position on a percentage basis. The Livermore ratio was 20%-20%-20%-40%. You may want to establish your own ratio.

Target Number of Shares

| PERCENTAGE | NUMBER | PRICE | DATE | $ AMOUNT |
|---|---|---|---|---|
| 20% | | | | |
| 20% | | | | |
| 20% | | | | |
| 40% | | | | |
| TOTAL | | | | |

### LIVERMORE MONEY MANAGEMENT RULE NUMBER TWO:

You should set a target as to how many shares you want to buy, what percentage of your portfolio you will invest in any single situation. The trader should also establish a general upside price target:

"I call this my *"Bucket Shop"* rule, because I learned it in the bucket shops where I worked all my trades with 10% margin. I was automatically sold out by the bucket shops if the loss exceeded the 10% limit. The 10% loss rule became my most important rule for managing money. It is also a key "timing" rule...since it automatically sets the time to exit a trade.

"Remember—a speculator must set a firm stop before making a trade and must: *NEVER SUSTAIN A LOSS OF MORE THAN 10% OF INVESTED CAPITAL!*

"IF YOU LOSE 50% YOU MUST GAIN 100% TO GET EVEN!"

#### LIVERMORE 10% LOSS TABLE

| STARTING POSITION | AMT LOST | REMAINDER | %LOSS | % TO RECOVER LOSS |
|---|---|---|---|---|
| $1000 | $80 | $920 | 8.0 | 8.7 |
| | 100 | 900 | 10.0 | 11.1 |
| | 200 | 800 | 20.0 | 25.0 |
| | 300 | 700 | 30.0 | 42.8 |
| | 400 | 600 | 40.0 | 66.6 |
| | 500 | 500 | 50.0 | 100.0 |

"I have also learned that when your broker calls you and tells you he needs more money for a margin requirement on a stock that is declining—tell him to sell out your position. When you buy a stock at 50 and it goes to 45, do not buy more in order to average out your price. The stock has not done what you predicted, that is enough of an indication that your judgment was wrong! Take your losses quickly and get out. Never meet a margin call, and never average losses.

"Many times I would close out a position before suffering a ten percent loss. I did this simply because the stock was not acting right from the start. Often my "instincts" would whisper to me— 'J. L., this stock has a malaise, it is a lagging dullard or just does not feel right,' and I would sell out my position in the beat of a bird's wing.

"Perhaps this was the "inner mind" working, distilling patterns and formations that I had seen thousands of times before, and sending subconscious signals, to my brain, unconsciously registering repeated patterns stored in my memory bank that were then subliminally remembered and awakened. Whatever it was, I have learned over the years through many market experiences, to respect these instincts.

"I absolutely believe that price movement patterns are being repeated; they are recurring patterns that appear over and over, with slight variations. This is because the stocks were being driven by humans—and human nature never changes.

"I have observed many times that people often become *'involuntary investors.'* They buy a stock that goes down, and they refuse to sell and take their loss. They prefer to hold on to the stock and hope that it will rally eventually and climb back up. This is why the 10% rule is essential. Don't ever become an *"involuntary investor."* Take your losses quickly! Easy to say—hard to do.

Livermore's mansion "Evermore" at King's Point Long Island. The dining room table sat 46 for dinner. There was a barbershop in the basement with a live-in barber. His 300-foot yacht was anchored in the back yard. The mansion was the scene of many grand parties—finally auctioned off—June 27th, 1933.

Daily News

Jesse Livermore and Ed Kelley, his friend, on Livermore's yacht after a day's fishing in the launch. Livermore had a passion for fishing. Being on the water gave him a chance to think. He often came up with "great market ideas" on the ocean.

Photo—Paul Livermore

The original *Anita Venetian* with a 40-foot launch tied along side. Livermore loved yachting. In all there were 3 *Anita Venetians*—the last one was 300 feet long.

Photo—Paul Livermore

Jesse and Dorothy March 3, 1926, looking dapper at a costume ball at their mansion "Evermore." Jesse Livermore loved beautiful women and his wife Dorothy loved throwing parties often for 100 people or more.

Photo—Daily News

The Breakers Hotel in Palm Beach on fire March 18th, 1925. Dorothy Livermore sent the bell boys back to the apartment to save her 24 pieces of Louis Vuitton luggage from the flames—and the bell boys did it. Two naked men can be seen in the foreground—they did not have time to put on their clothes.

Photo—Palm Beach Historical Society

Bradley's Palm Beach "Beach Club"—the longest-running illegal gambling casino in America's history. Ed Bradley, the "greatest gambler" in America, and Jesse Livermore, the "greatest stock speculator" in America, were fast friends.

Photo—Palm Beach Historical Society

Paul Livermore, Dorothy Livermore, and Jesse Junior in front of the Livermore mansion. Both sons were very handsome. Jesse Jr., started having sex with his mother's friends—without her knowledge—when he was fourteen—the same age he started drinking.

Photo—Corbis Bettman Archive

Jesse Livermore stands on the porch of the Breakers Hotel in Palm Beach where he took a large apartment every winter. He traveled to the Breakers in his private railway car and had his yacht sent down to Palm Beach ahead of his arrival.

Photo—Corbis Bettman Archive

Jesse Livermore, Dorothy Livermore and friends at their vacation home in Lake Placid. Livermore hunted and played golf here.

Photo—Paul Livermore

Dorothy Livermore and a friend in a white wicker Pedi-cab on the grounds of the Breakers Hotel. This was a common means of transportation at the "Breakers" in the twenties and thirties.

Photo—Patricia Livermore

Patricia and Jesse Livermore Jr.—during their happy times on the way to Hawaii. Jesse Jr. would later fall into deep alcoholism and physically abuse Patricia until he finally tried to kill her.

Photo—Patricia Livermore

Jesse Livermore loved beautiful women. This caused him much grief during his life. He is pictured here with his third wife Harriet during a party for eighty people in their ten-room apartment on Park Avenue.

Photo—Corbis Bettman Archive

Publicity photo of the handsome Paul Livermore, Jesse's youngest son. He appeared in a number of movies and various television series before moving to Hawaii.

Photo—Paul Livermore

The beautiful Ann Livermore, Paul's wife—she is a singer who appeared with the big bands, and such singers as Tony Bennett and Frank Sinatra. She still sings in her home town—Las Vegas.

Photo—Ann Livermore

Jesse Livermore, third wife Harriet, and his son Paul—as they arrive in New York on December 8, 1935, after leaving the bedside of Jesse Jr., who had just been shot by his mother.

Photo—Daily News

After shooting her son, Dorothy Livermore stands in a Santa Barbara, California courtroom waiting to be arraigned. She is before Judge Ernest Wagner on a complaint of assault with a deadly weapon with intent to kill.

Photo—Corbis Bettman Archive

Jesse Livermore Jr., March 23, 1975, as he is led from his home to police car after shooting his dog, attempting to kill his wife Patricia, and sticking his gun in the chest of a NYPD police officer and pulling the trigger.

Photo—Daily News

Under Sheriff Jack Ross, District Attorney Percy Heckendorf and Sheriff James Ross are looking at the spot they believe Jesse Livermore Jr. was shot by his mother in her home in Montecito, California. He was actually shot on the staircase.

Photo—Corbis Bettman Archive

Jesse Livermore sits before the bankruptcy referee on May 15, 1934. Livermore always paid his bankruptcy creditors back when he got back on his feet, even though he was not legally responsible.

Photo—Daily News

Jesse Livermore "The Boy Plunger" of Wall Street and his wife of twenty months set sail to Europe on the S.S. Rex after his 1934 bankruptcy. Before boarding Livermore said, "I hope to relieve my mind of some of my troubles."

Photo—Daily News

Jesse Livermore and his wife Harriet on November 27, 1940, at the Stork Club, Livermore's favorite night club. Looking distant, pale and wan, he would commit suicide the next day.

Photo—Daily News

November 28, 1940—Jesse Livermore Jr., as he arrives at the Sherry Netherland Hotel in New York to identify the body of his father. On viewing his father's body, minutes later, he collapsed.

Photo—Daily News

Livermore was subject to deep black depressions all his adult life, during success or failure. This photo was taken on November 26, 1940, two days before "The Great Bear" of Wall Street took his own life.

Photo—Corbis Bettman Archive

Jesse Livermore was a handsome and powerful man who cherished his secrecy and his private life. He moved in silence and mystery and was like catnip to women.

Photo—Paul Livermore

"My early days of trading in the "Bucket Shops," where a person would be wiped out as soon as his margin was exceeded, caused me to develop my 10% rule—if I lost more than ten percent on a trade I would sell immediately. I never asked for the reason the fact that it had dropped was reason enough to get out. I would also sell on instinct, which really wasn't instinct it was the cumulative consciousness of years of playing the market. If I bought a stock with a certain scenario in mind for what I expected the stock to do—well, if it did not follow through with the expected scenario and go up immediately, I often just went ahead and sold it automatically—I had bought on the expectation that the stock would do something and it did not do what I expected—often that was enough evidence for me to sell the stock. I also never looked back—I had no recriminations for myself, or bitter thoughts, if the stock later took off.

I later in life developed my theory on the importance of the dimension of time in trading the stock market. By moving quickly, I avoided those situations where a stock just sits in a channel for a long period of time and your money becomes inactive. Like a person who owns a retail store and one item just sits on the shelf, stagnant. The smart retailer "clears out" that item, and uses the money to stock an item that sells, an item that is in demand.

The same is true of the stock market, keep your money invested in the leaders, the stocks that are moving. Time is a true trading dimension in operating in the stock market.

## LIVERMORE MONEY MANAGEMENT RULE NUMBER THREE:

"Keep a cash reserve. The successful speculator must always have cash in reserve, like a good general who keeps troops in reserve for exactly the right moment, and then moves with great conviction, and commits his reserve armies for the final crushing victory, because he has waited for all the factors to be right, until all the odds are in his favor.

"There is a never ending stream of opportunities in the stock market, and if you miss a good opportunity, wait a little while, be patient, and another one will come along. Don't reach for a trade, 'ALL' the conditions for a good trade must be on your side. Remember that you do not have to be in the market all the time.

"I like to use the analogy of playing cards—for me it was poker, and bridge; it is only human nature to want to play every hand. This desire to *"always be in the game,"* is one of the speculator's greatest enemies in managing his money. It will eventually bring about disaster, as it has brought bankruptcy and financial disaster to me several times in my early career.

*"THERE ARE TIMES WHEN PLAYING THE STOCK MARKET THAT YOUR MONEY SHOULD BE INACTIVE—WAITING ON THE SIDELINES IN CASH—WAITING TO COME INTO PLAY—IN THE STOCK MARKET—TIME IS NOT MONEY—TIME IS TIME—AND MONEY IS MONEY.*

*"OFTEN MONEY THAT IS JUST SITTING CAN LATER BE MOVED INTO THE RIGHT SITUATION AT THE RIGHT TIME AND MAKE A VAST FORTUNE –PATIENCE –PATIENCE–PATIENCE IS THE KEY TO SUCCESS NOT SPEED–TIME IS A CUNNING SPECULATOR'S BEST FRIEND IF HE USES IT RIGHT."*

"Remember the clever speculator is always patient and has a reserve of cash."

## LIVERMORE MONEY MANAGEMENT RULE NUMBER FOUR:

"Stick with the winners—as long as the stock is acting right—do not be in a hurry to take a profit. You must know you are right in your basic judgment, or you would have no profit at all. If there is nothing basically negative—well then —Let it ride! It may grow into a very large profit, as long as the action of the overall market and the stock does not give you cause to worry, let it ride—have the courage of your convictions. Stay with it!

"When I was in profit on a trade I was never nervous. I could have a line of a hundred thousand shares out on a single stock play and sleep like a baby. Why? Because I was in profit on that trade. I was simply *"USING THE TRACK'S MONEY—THE STOCK MARKET'S MONEY,"* and if I lost all this profit—well then I had lost money I never had in the first place.

"Of course, the opposite is true, if I bought a stock and it went against me I would sell it immediately. You can't stop and try to figure out "WHY" it is going in the wrong direction—the fact that it "IS" going in the wrong direction and that is enough evidence for an experienced speculator to close the trade.

"Profits take care of themselves—losses never do.

"Never confuse this approach of letting the position ride with the 'buy and hold forever' strategy. I do not and never have blindly bought and held a stock. How can we know that far into the future? Things change: life changes, relationships change, health changes, seasons change, your children change, your lover changes, why shouldn't the basic conditions that originally caused you to buy a stock change? To buy and hold blindly on the basis that it is a great company, or a strong industry, or the economy's generally healthy, is, to me, the equivalent of stock-market suicide.

"One of my most important points in buying a stock was to try and buy as closely as possible to the Reversal Pivotal Point or the Continuation Pivotal Point. It was from this point that my key decisions were made. If the stock advanced from the Reversal Pivotal Points I would hold it and relax, because from that point on I was playing with the house's money, not my own capital. If the stock pulled away from the Pivotal Point in the opposite direction of my purchase I would automatically sell. Once in the green I was totally relaxed and just observed the stock's movements in total calm and did nothing until it was time to close the trade. The possibility of losing my "paper profits" never bothered me, since it was not my money to begin with. It therefore became my biggest job to find the Reversal Pivotal Points and Continuation Pivotal Points. The rule: cut your losses—let your profits run.

"Stick with the winners—let them ride until you have a clear reason to sell."

## LIVERMORE MONEY MANAGEMENT RULE NUMBER FIVE:

Livermore: "I recommended parking fifty percent of your profits from a successful trade, especially where you doubled your original capital. Set this money aside, put it in the bank, hold it in reserve, or lock it up in a safe deposit box.

"Like winning in the casino, it's a good idea, now and then, to take your winnings off the table, and turn them into cash. There is no better time then after a large "win" on a stock. Cash is your secret bullet in the chamber, keep a cash reserve.

"The single largest regret I have ever had in my financial life was not paying enough attention to this rule."

## AVOID CHEAP STOCKS

"One of the greatest mistakes that even experienced investors make is in buying cheap securities, just because they are selling at a low price. While it may happen that in some instances stock demand pushes the stock from a small digit price of say five or ten dollars a share to over a hundred dollars, many of these low priced stocks later sink into oblivion by going into receivership, or else they struggle for years and years, with only the slightest prospects of ever returning a profit to their shareholders.

"In selecting securities, it is essential for an investor to determine which industries—groups are in the strongest disposition, which are less strong and which groups are comparatively weak, very weak, etc. The speculator should not plunge into cheap stocks in depressed industry groups—just because the stock may appear as a bargain. Stay with the powerful healthy Industry Groups.

"Keep your funds liquid and working for you! Perhaps nothing has so interfered with the proverbial poor success of the public in the investment markets as this fact—that it does not keep its investment and speculative funds in proper circulation. The public is usually in a permanent loaded-up or tied-up condition, with no cash or buying power in reserve.

"Tell the public that a certain stock may advance a few points a month and do you find them interested? No, they want something that moves more quickly. Yet in a few months they will probably wake up to see the stocks they refused selling for 20 points higher, while their cheap, volatile stocks, which they actually purchased, selling at less than the prices they paid for them.

## DISREGARD THE ACTION OF INSIDERS

"I never pay any attention to the actions of insiders, the directors and the management. Insiders are commonly the absolute worst judges of their own stock. They know too much about their stocks and they are too close to observe their weaknesses. Key executives are also usually ignorant about the stock market, especially market technical indicators and group movement. They are often reluctant to admit that the stock market is an entirely different business than the business they are engaged in. In other words, you can be an expert in radio broadcasting or automobiles, or the manufacture of steel, and still not know anything about trading stocks, especially in a volatile stock market.

"Often I have observed that the Chief Executive Officer of most companies is little more than a cheerleader, who has only one job with regard to the market. He must assure and reassure the shareholders that everything is fine—if sales are down he tells the shareholders that the decline in sales is nothing more than a slight problem due to some temporary reason. If profits are down he assures the shareholders there is nothing to worry about since the company has already reacted and made adequate plans to recapture their profitability.

## ESTABLISH A PROFIT TARGET — RISK REWARD RATIO

"I also paid a lot of attention to the ratio of my potential profit and the size of my investment. If a stock was trading at $200 and I expected a 20-point move or 10% I deduced that I would have to put up $200,000 to make $20,000. This was not appealing for me because the risk/reward ratio was out of balance. No matter how good a trader you are, losses are inevitable in the stock market and must be considered as part of your trading operating expenses, along with interest, brokerage fees, and capital gain tax. It was my experience that few investors established a risk/reward ratio before they entered a trade. It is essential to try and do this, have a specific plan.

"I was a lot less active in my trading than people thought I was. In my later life I was only interested in the 'essential move,' the important swing in the price of the stock. This often took much "patience" in waiting for all the factors to come together into a focal point where I felt as much as possible that everything was in my favor, the direction of the overall market, the industry group, the sister stock activity and finally the timing was correct and an important Pivotal Point was reached.

"When I said it was the 'sittin and the waitin' that was important I did not mean AFTER the stock was purchased I meant BEFORE the stock was purchased—that's when you have to sit and wait for all factors to come together to merge into the perfect trade, or as perfect as possible. My personal rule: Make sure that you have placed as many factors in your favor as possible and never RUSH into any trade, take your time, there will always be another play. Remember, it is very difficult to work your way back from a devastating loss—this is true no matter what anyone tells you. Take it from a man who knows, as I said; like a merchant with no inventory–that's a stock trader with no cash—out of business. So, have patience—go slow—don't risk all your capital in any one situation—protect it—the only exception is when you are playing with the "House's Money" the capital made directly from the market–from that stock.

## ALWAYS ESTABLISH A STOP BEFORE MAKING A TRADE

"When you purchase a stock you should have a clear target where to sell if the stock moves against you. And you must obey your rules! Never sustain a loss of more than ten percent of your invested capital. Losses are twice as expensive to make up.

"And you must obey your rules...no cheating, by procrastination, by waiting! My basic rule was, never take more than a ten-percent loss of capital.

"I always established a stop before making the trade. Another reason for buying on the Pivotal Point is that it always gave me a clear point of reference. If it was a Pivotal Point on the top or the bottom of a move or a breakout to a new high Pivotal Point or if it was a breakout from a consolidation or as I called them: a Continuation Pivotal Point I then had a reference point to select as a point for my STOP, where I would close my trade if things went against me. Most stock traders do not take the time to do the following:

*Decide on the potential of the trade versus the size of the investment—if it is a large investment with a small potential return, then pass.

*Before you buy, make sure that you are buying at a crucial Pivotal Point and use this as the spot to establish your exit point if the trade goes bad—write this down and honor it—cut your losses—this is the most important thing, even if you get whipsawed and it rallies right back. It did not do what you expected it to do—this is the most important thing to remember.

*Make sure all things are in your favor, market direction, group direction, sister stock direction and the exact timing is in place.

*Once this has been done the trader must then assume the status of an automaton, a robot, and he must then follow his rules.

"I hope this does not offend the reader but the general public is usually not successful in trading their own accounts. The general public will sit still for a five point gain and a ten point loss. They will assume that this is nothing but a normal reaction and they will sit through this drop. In the beginning of a trade I watch the stock as closely as possible, because I have hopefully waited to buy it on a breakout. If it does not breakout or in fact goes in the opposite direction, then I will immediately get out of the stock.

"Why? It's simple, the stock did not do what I expected it to do, therefore my judgment was wrong, never mind "Why" it was wrong—the fact is that it "Was" wrong so I must get out of the position. Remember, I know that a certain number of trades will be wrong and so I do not think about them or blame myself—no, I usually move on to a new situation—I say usually because sometimes I have found that I was just too early in my overall assessment and I then sit in cash and wait.

"Remember that no Trader's judgment is infallible, if it were always correct that person would soon be the richest man on this planet. But it is not the case—we all make mistakes and we will continue to make mistakes in our lives and in the Stock Market! The rewards can be enormous if we can learn to *'cut the losses quickly and let the profits ride'*—do not sell a stock unless you have a good reason—just simply wanting to take the profit is usually not a good enough reason.

## TIME AS A TRADING DIMENSION

"Later in my trading history, I decided that I would not hold stocks that did not move in the direction I had anticipated. I would wait for what I considered to be the perfect time to buy the stock, if it did not move as I believed it should move within a few days or what I considered a reasonable time, say a week or two, I would then sell out the position. I would wait days, weeks, months, for the stock to position itself at the spot I thought most opportune, in other words the perfect moment to make my purchase—when every factor was in my favor. If the stock did not do as expected I would often sell my position, even if the stock did not decline.

The one thing I learned in my many years of playing the stock market is that there are always opportunities in the market, so to remain with your cash in a stand-by position meant that your money, your inventory, was inactive now but this could yield huge benefits in the future, when it was finally committed to that "special situation." Just as it is true that many people will sell their good stocks and keep their losers it is true that they will also keep the stocks that are flat, not doing anything, or going anywhere.

"Please beware that this does not mean a stock will not have a normal correction or a normal consolidation in an upward trend...what we are talking about here is a stock that is just wallowing in a trading channel making no progress in either direction is the stock being accumulated or is it being distributed. If it is not clear then it is sometimes best to exit the stock than to take a chance that it is being distributed and will eventually go down and cost you money. Give the stock a little time to show itself in these situations, but waste no time in closing out an inconclusive stock and moving on to another trading situation.

"I have often sold a stock that has moved a point or two in my favor, but I simply do not like the weak or limp manner in which the stock is acting. It does not matter to me if I am even, or a have a small profit or a small loss–the facts remain–the stock did not do what I had analyzed and believed that it would do—so the conclusion is always simple to me—my judgment was wrong and I must exit the trade. One thing I know for sure is that my judgment has been wrong in the past and it will be wrong again in the future. The DANGER is in not recognizing it and getting out. The wise are right—pride often does come before a fall.

"The worse kinds of stocks are what I call **'Listless Drifters'** these are stocks that do not move in the desired manner and simply tie up a stock market trader's capital as they hang out there drifting in no man's land. Whenever I have had to depend on hope I have always felt exposed to danger. When I have taken my loss I know what it is and I know what I have to make back to get into profit. Also if I stay with my losing position or listless position, it has always bothered me in moving ahead with future trades. I have discovered that I cannot afford to trade in anything but live stocks, stocks that are leading the pack, stocks that have inherent energy. This energy and momentum has always meant I trade on both sides of the market—the upside and the downside, long or short."

"I have observed many, many people who have purchased stocks and put them away in safe deposit boxes or in safes, feeling that their investment is also safe. This is never true, one can never assume that a stock can be bought and put away for the future; the good thoughts that people had for Steel, Radio, Aircraft, Oil, Railroads, and hundreds of other safe as *"money in the bank"* securities over the year that all went sour.

"I believe in keeping my capital in circulation. Remember, when a merchant has part of his capital "frozen" out of circulation he must then make all his profit on the capital that is left not "frozen" this hampers and hinders him because that *"unfrozen capital"* must often work twice as hard to make up for the *"dead-frozen"* capital which yields little or nothing.

"But above and beyond this reasoning are what I call "lost opportunities" because their capital is frozen these stock traders miss many golden opportunities to trade the winners, the stocks that would have bought them profits and success—profits that were unavailable because their capital was tied up in stagnant, unprofitable situations.

"Hope is the villain here and it has ruined millions of speculators over the course of time—take your losses right away they are real whether you sell the stocks or not.

"To put this in another way I have two stops in mind when I enter a trade I have a "PRICE STOP" and I have a "TIME STOP." I will not stay with any trade more than a few points if it moves against me and I will not stay with a stock position for more than a few days if the stock does not perform as I expect it to perform.

"This is the lifeblood of my trading technique because it is how I keep my capital in working circulation. It may sound contradictory, but it isn't, there are times when I am out of the market completely with all my working capital in cash, waiting and waiting for the market to choose a trend and for the perfect trading scenario to present itself to me. For a key to the market is to always have that cash reserve that you can call into action, like a general holding his final army in reserve, waiting to commit it to battle at the perfect moment to insure victory.

## POINTS ARE A KEY TO MONEY MANAGEMENT

"I wanted at least the opportunity of a ten point gain in any stock I invested in. My rule:

**'Stick to the strongest industries and pick out the strongest stocks in those industry groups.'**

"I have always considered the "points" as the key in my trading. I have no prejudice for cheap stocks or expensive stocks and I know that if a stock goes from 10 dollars to 20 dollars it is a 100% gain whereas a stock that goes from 100 to 200 is a hundred point gain, as well as a 100% increase in value.

"The main challenge is to identify the current leaders and to spot the new leaders who are waiting to take over from the current existing leaders. During major shifts and changes in market direction it is of paramount importance to observe the leaders that are being driven out and identify the new leading stocks that will assume the leadership in the future.

"It is also my observation that it is usually always best to go with the strongest stock in the strongest group—do not look for the cheapest or the laggard stock that has not yet had his turn to move in the group—always go for the strongest most dominant stock in the group.

## LIVERMORE'S METHOD OF PYRAMIDING

"I learned from many experienced old hands in the market and from my own experience that: *'You Never Average Down.'* That is, if the stock you bought goes down in price—DO NOT BUY ANY MORE and try to average your price—it hardly ever works. But what does often work is *'Averaging up'* in price—BUYING MORE AS THE STOCK GOES UP IN PRICE. But I have found this can be dangerous also, so I have tried to establish my main position at the beginning, at the initial Pivotal Point, and then increase it at what I call the Continuation Pivotal Point—providing the stock comes out of the consolidation with strength. By this I mean the trader must wait until the stock has proven it is going to break out on the strong side of the Continuation Pivotal Point and the trader must not anticipate this, because until the stock declares itself, it is always a risk. At these junctures the trader must watch like a hawk and stay "poised" but not "biased" by hope.

"The final time a trader can pyramid is when a stock breaks out to a clear new high on HEAVY VOLUME this is a very good sign because it most likely means that there is no more overhanging stock to stop the progress of the stock for a while.

7-15-99        CAPITAL ONE FINANCIAL CORP (COF)        48.93

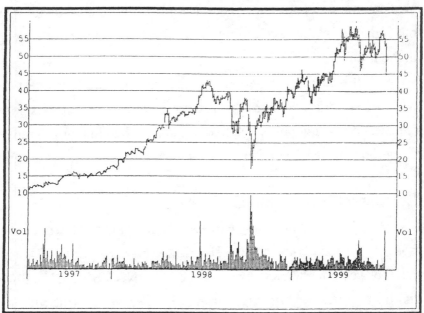

*Note Example: Capital One Financials' terrific volume, and spike down, in early October shows a clear "high-volume climax-bottom" that indicates the downward trend has changed. Be alert that VOLUME is often a key confirming signal to indicate a change in direction.*

"Pyramiding is a dangerous activity and anyone who tries it must be very agile and experienced, for the further a stock gets extended in its rise or decline the more dangerous the situation becomes. I tried to restrict any serious pyramiding to the beginning of the move. I found it not wise to enter a pyramiding action if the stock was far from the base—better to wait for the Continuation Pivotal Point of the breakout from a new high.

"Always remember there are no ironclad rules to the stock market, the main objective for the stock speculator is to try and place as many factors in his favor as he can. And even with this in place the trader will still be wrong on many occasions and he must react by cutting his losses.

"The following rule is a rule I developed from a great trader: Keep stress at bay—act in all ways to keep the mind clear and your judgment correct. I did all I could to achieve this in my physical life by going to bed early, eating and drinking lightly, taking exercise, standing upright at the stock ticker, standing while on the telephone and demanding silence in the office. I spoke to no one on my way to work and kept silent about my stock market actions.

"But I still think one of the greatest things for a speculator is to keep some cash in reserve for those incredible moments in trading the market when all the factors come together to form the 'Supreme Trade at the Perfect Moment' such as occur at the Zenith of Bull Markets and the Nadir's of panics. There is no better feeling than having a strong army of cash standing by waiting to move into action."

## PROFITS: THE SPINE OF EVERY STOCK

"There is no magic about achieving success in the stock market. The only way I know for anyone to succeed in his investments is for him to investigate before he invests; to look before he leaps; to stick to the fundamentals of his rules, and disregard everything else.

"As I have often said, no person can succeed in the stock market unless he or she acquires a fundamental knowledge of economics and thoroughly familiarizes himself with conditions of every sort—the financial position of a company, its past history, production capabilities, as well as the state of the industry in which the company is engaged, and the overall general economic situation.

"In the end, it is earnings—profits, and profit potential that moves stock, not emotions, like hope and greed. In the final analysis, it is profits, real and imagined, that eventually drive the price of stocks and remember that reality will always eventually set in to produce a final conclusion for the industry group and any particular stock."

## Chapter 10

# JESSE LIVERMORE
## How To Trade In Stocks

### Emotional Control

Livermore had been actively trading for 32 years by 1923. He was 46 years old. He had an unquenchable thirst for knowledge about his chosen profession, and he was a constant student of the technical side of the market. He was also a great student of the psychology of the market. At one point he took psychology courses at night school to better understand human nature. Livermore concluded that there may be millions of minds at work in the market, but there was basically only a few psychological patterns that had to be studied and understood—since human nature has common traits.

Later in his life he was asked an important question by his sons, Paul and Jesse Jr., "Dad, why are you good in the market and other people lose all their money?"

"Well boys, I have also lost money, but each time I lost, I tried to learn why I had lost. The stock market must be studied, not in a casual way, but in a deep knowledgeable way. It's my conclusion that most people pay more care and attention to the purchase of an appliance for their house, or in buying a car, than they do to the purchase of stocks. The stock market, with its allure of easy money, and fast action induces people into foolishness and the careless handling of their hard earned money, like no other entity.

"You see, the purchase of a stock is simple, easily done by placing your purchase order with a broker, and later a phone call to sell, completes the trade. If you profit from this transaction it appears to be easy money with seemingly no work. You didn't have to get to work by nine and labor for eight hours a day. It was simply a paper transaction, requiring what appears to be no labor. It gives the clear appearance of an easy way to get rich. Simply buy the stock at 10 dollars and sell it later for more than 10 dollars. The more you trade, the more you made, that's how it appears. Simply put, it's ignorance.

"And you must constantly deal with your emotions—there's fear to deal with, which you will find out when you grow up. Fear lies buried just beneath the surface of all normal human life. Fear, like violence, can appear in a single heartbeat, a fast breath, a blink of the eye, the grab of a hand, the noise of a gun. When it appears, natural survival tactics come alive, normal reasoning is distorted. Reasonable people act unreasonably when they are afraid. And people become afraid when they start to lose money, their judgment becomes impaired. This is our human nature in this stage of our evolution. It cannot be denied. It must be understood, particularly in trading the market.

"And the unsuccessful investor is best friends with hope—and hope skips along life's path hand-in-hand with greed and fear when it comes to the stock market. Once a stock trade is entered, hope springs to life. It is man's nature to be hopeful, to be positive, to hope for the best.

Hope is an important survival technique for the human race. But hope, like it's stock market cousins: ignorance, greed and fear, all distort reason. See boys, the stock market only deals in facts, in reality, in reason, and the stock market is never wrong—traders are wrong. Like the spinning of a roulette wheel, the little black ball tells the final outcome, not greed, fear, or hope. The result is objective and final, with no appeal, like pure nature."

Both boys wondered if the stock market was for them. Was it too dangerous? Should they just leave it to their father.

Livermore went on: "I believe that the public wants to be led, to be instructed, to be told what to do. They want reassurance. They will always move en masse, a mob, a herd, a group, because people want the safety of human company. They are afraid to stand-alone because the belief is that it is safer to be included within the herd, not to be the lone calf standing on the desolate, dangerous wolf-patrolled prairie of contrary opinion—and the truth is that it usually "is" safer to go with the trend.

"This is where it gets slightly complicated. I always wanted to trade along the *LINE OF LEAST RESISTANCE—THE TREND,* so I was generally moving along with the crowd, the herd, most of the time. It was when the *'change in trend'* started to appear the change in overall market direction that was the most difficult moment to catch and act upon. I always was hunting for the clues to the change. But, I was always ready to separate myself from the popular thinking, the group thinking and go in the opposite direction, because I believed in cycles—like life they go up and down.

"The change in trend is the most difficult time in a speculator's trading life. These major changes in trends were hell. But, I did not want to toboggan downhill with the crowd, unless I had sold stocks short.

"With this in mind, I developed two rules that I followed.

"First: do not be invested in the market all the time—there are many times when I have been completely in cash, especially when I was unsure of the direction of the market and waiting for a confirmation of the next move. In my later life, whenever I deduced that a change was coming, and I wasn't sure exactly when, or how severe the change might be, I cashed in all my positions and waited.

"Second: it is the change in the major trend that hurts most speculators. They simply get caught invested in the wrong direction, on the wrong side of the market. To determine if I was right in my appraisal that a change in market trend was coming I used *SMALL POSITION PROBES*, placing small orders, either buy or sell orders depending on the direction of the trend change, to test the correctness of my judgment, by sending out exploratory orders and investing real money I usually got the signal that the trend was changing because each stock purchase was at a cheaper price than the prior purchase—the prices were dropping.

## How Livermore Prepared for His Day

Jesse Livermore was a highly disciplined man. During the week, he went to bed every night at 10 P.M. and arose each morning at six. He preferred to have no one around him for the first hour. The kitchen staff was trained to leave his coffee and juice on the table in the solarium if he was in his mansion at Great Neck, Long Island. The newspapers were also laid out for him, including the European and Chicago newspapers. He read voraciously all his life. He wanted this hour or two to plan his day. Livermore had observed that few men really planned their day. Yes, they were organized, they had appointments scheduled, lunch engagements, and public affairs planned and written down. They knew in detail what awaited them, meetings, and people coming by the office, phone calls they would make and receive. They knew what had been planned for them—but what items of major importance had they planned actually to get done for themselves.

Livermore, on special occasions, spoke to his sons of his business, in his massive library in the house on Long Island: "Boys, you will find that hardly any businessman really plans his day to handle the most important items. In most cases his day is laid out for him-organized for him by his secretary and his staff. He is merely an attending party. At the completion of the day he is often left with the most important matters still unattended, unexamined, uncompleted. Important strategy matters in running a complex business are perhaps not being attended: personnel problems, mergers and acquisitions, raising capital, and great marketing concepts—like buying on the installment plan was to banking—or perhaps the competition is not being clearly examined or assessed.

"Not so for me. In the stock market, my moves must be based as much on clear facts as they can be. To play the market properly requires silence, and seclusion to examine the situation, and to appraise, and deliberate on new information that comes to hand during the trading day. One must always have a clear strategy to play the market.

"I have found that it is easy to pick up the phone and pull the trigger by buying or selling. The problem is knowing when and what to do and to follow religiously your own rules.

"Boys, I decided long ago that if there are going to be mistakes made in my trading—I want them to be *'my mistakes.'* I don't need someone else to lose my money for me by giving me tips, or influencing my trades. In the business I am in there is no room for post-mortems, you either make money or you lose money...or your money just sits there waiting for the right situation while earning small interest.

"That's why I go to bed at ten and rise at six. The careful, disciplined man must be aware of everything, ignorant of nothing. You can not afford to be careless about anything. Sometimes overlooking a single item, big or small, can ruin everything, kill all your plans. Like a General in wartime, his men's lives depend on his thoroughness in planning and executing that plan. In the stock market there is no room for error and carelessness.

"People think that I am simply a speculator, a trader, who finds situations and plunges into them. Nothing could be further from the truth. I often pick up small seemingly useless clues in the newspapers and after checking them out, investigating what is behind them, I will act upon them.

"You ask about my day? In the solitude of the morning hours, after being rejuvenated from sleep, with nothing to distract me, I carefully read the papers. I have often used small specific news items like weather events, like droughts, insect problems, labor strikes, and assess how they would effect the corn, wheat or cotton yields that often lead me to generalities, and a possible trade.

"I got my news on the financial side by examining the actual prices and actions in the commodities market such as: coal, copper, steel, textiles, sugar, corn wheat, automobile sales, and employment figures. I got a feel and a correct judgment on general business conditions in the United States. It was no one single fact, it was a plethora of facts that finally led me down a narrow path to a trade.

"I did more than just scan the headlines of the newspaper, I read the paper carefully looking for small items of news that might provide me with important clues especially about an industry group or a specific stock that had changed from weak to strong or vice-versa.

"The headlines are for the suckers. A good speculator has to get behind the news and see what was really going on. Beware, often misleading articles are planted by people or brokers with hidden agendas, who want to sell their stock on the good news or they want to keep people invested while they go ahead and distribute their own stock.

"Once I traveled in my railway car to Pittsburgh where I observed that the steel mills were not at 30 percent capacity, they were at less than 20 percent and falling. In other words, they were a perfect short sale.

"Unfortunately many people who invest in the market only read the headlines and they too easily believe what they read. This is unfortunate since there are many pitfalls, schemes, and dangers, slick money traps always appear wherever great sums of money are involved, such as the stock market. It is my observation that often what you read in the newspaper is nothing more than another form of a stock tip—so the reader has to beware of the source, motives and effect of what he is reading on the stock market, otherwise chances are he or she will become a sucker too.

"Boys, it is my observation that there is no better time than the early morning to gain an enormous advantage toward being a successful stock trader. There is silence in the house, no person or thing is disturbing your concentration, and the mind is renewed after a good night's sleep.

"You will learn as you grow older that most people simply get up at a certain time in the morning, get ready and go directly to the office. Often, these same people feel the desire to go out at night during the week to the cinema, a play, a long dinner with several drinks. In other words, they feel the need for social interaction or recreation during the weekdays. This may work well in other fields of endeavor, but it is a dangerous practice on a regular basis if a person wants to be successful in seriously trading the stock market. A good stock trader is not unlike a well-trained professional athlete who must keep the physical side of their life in perfect form if they want to continue to be at the top of their mental form. The body must be in tune with the mind, for there is no more intense or exciting field of battle than the stock market. A person is making a mistake if they think success in the stock market comes easily, instantly, or steadily without great effort. The successful trader must always be in top physical form.

"During the week I have always been willing to sacrifice the diversions offered to people from ten o'clock at night until two in the morning. I do not feel I have missed anything by being asleep during this period and up at five or six in the morning. I have found for me that there is true joy in the solitude and pure work I did during this time, all my life. For, I always believed I was in search of bigger game, than just pleasure and social interaction. I wanted to be supreme in my endeavors in the stock market—this is what gave me real pleasure and satisfaction. Playing the game and winning the game.

"Finally, it has been my observation that the public believe the stock market is an easy way to make money. They have some extra money to invest and they believe the stock market should offer them an easy way to increase the value of the money that they have invested.

"This is not the case. I have observed that people who have no knowledge of the stock market, but insist on playing the stock market, generally lose their money in a hurry.

"So I believe that if you want to succeed in the stock market make sure you get plenty of sleep, and give yourself plenty of time for the uninterrupted study of all the elements involved with the stock market and remember that the essential to success in the stock market is knowledge and patience. So few people succeed in the market because they have no patience and are generally ignorant of the market and finally they want to get rich quickly.

"Anyone who figures that his success is dependent upon chance may as well stay out of the market. His attitude is wrong from the very start. The great trouble with the average person who buys securities is that they think the market is a gambling proposition.

"One should realize at the outset that to work in the stock market requires the same study and preparation as law or medicine. Certain rules of the stock market are to be studied as closely as if he were a law student preparing for the bar. Many people attribute my success to luck. That is not true; the fact is that since I was fifteen, I have studied this subject closely. I have given my life to it, concentrating upon it and putting into it my very best."

## THE SPECIAL ARRANGEMENT OF HIS OFFICE

"My main objective was to protect myself from unwelcomed bad influences—in particular I was trying to avoid anyone who might be inclined to offer me assistance in trading the stock market by giving me some information—in the form of a tip. Tips were the one thing that had done me the most harm in trading the stock market.

"I never wanted to be part of a group of stock market traders especially those traders who gathered in the brokerage office. My main reason was that I needed continuity of thought. I needed to be able to have more than 15 minutes of uninterrupted thought. Tips, gossip, and the interpretation of the daily news events concerning the stock market by the people gathered in an office held no interest for me.

"In the larger brokerage offices where a large number of people gathered was chaos to my brain. As far as I was concerned, it was hurtful to my trading, to be with these people, with their own biases and their own hidden agendas which did not necessarily match up with my own. I believed in working in silence and keeping my own council. As a friend of mind once told me, I do not take tips. I prefer to make my own mistakes not the mistakes of other people!' As far as I am concerned my friend was right.

"I also travel from my home to my offices undisturbed. I either travel to the office by car in silence and isolation or by my boat in the better weather, also in silence, with no other passengers—this gives me a chance to read the newspaper and plan my day. I do this to avoid meeting people who'll eventually inquire about the stock market, the subject comes up almost automatically. I am then forced to listen to tips, gossip, and prognostications that will inevitably creep into my conscious and sub-conscious mind and therefore affect my judgment. If I travel by myself I can continue with my thinking without any interference in implementing my plan for the day. I agree with my friend Bernard Baruch who tells his brokers: 'If you know anything about the stock I am trading...please do not tell me.'

"I believe that one of the most important qualifications for a successful trader is "POISE" which to me is defined as stability, a well balanced person with dignity of manner—as it relates to the stock market. A poised person is a person who can handle their hopes and their fears in a calm manner. The other qualification is "PATIENCE" to wait for the opportune time, when as many factors as possible are positioned in the traders favor. Poise and patience are the close friends of successful traders.

The final qualification is "SILENCE." Keep your own silent counsel—keep your victories and your failures to yourself—learn from them both. Poise, Patience, and Silence are attributes that must be cultivated. These virtues do not come automatically to the stock market trader.

"I was often the first one to the office followed by Harry Dache my office manager and security manager. The board men, usually six in total, filed into the office by nine o'clock to take their positions on the chalk board to file the trades as they occurred. For volume numbers I consulted the actual ticker tape. I positioned the main ticker in the center of the board on a tall podium so all I had to do was raise or lower my eyes to see the action of stocks I owned or was interested in. I also employed telephone lines that went directly to the "hot" posts I was trading at the time, say steel, motors, mail order or radio. I used the largest and fastest ticker tape and positioned it at near eye level so it was easily accessible. In fact, I generally used "tall ticker tapes" so that I had to stand while I read the tape. Standing in an erect position insured me of proper blood circulation, and better breathing. I found this helped to keep me calm during stressful trading periods. I am up and on my feet nearly all the time that the market is open. This gave me a little exercise and kept my senses at a higher pitch. The bent-over or lounging position was never a position I wanted to assume. I consider the market a great challenge that demands total concentration and is not for the lazy, even my telephoning I did from a standing position.

"I also allowed "No Talking" once the bell rang. I wanted silence in the office while the market was open. My phone number was known to very few people and I would often change it to keep people from reaching me. I received as little mail as possible and I answered as little mail as possible during the working day. I only am interested in the stock market; it is my sole job and I consider all else as an unwelcome distraction from my job.

"One of the things I liked best about my job, after I had fallen into many pitfalls and managed to climb out, was the solitude—I loved the individuality, being the lone wolf—the solitude—everything that happened occurred as a result of my judgment.

"I had no interest in sharing my market experiences with anyone—the good or the bad. I couldn't. After all, how could they care, it had nothing to do with their lives. And I had come to know by then that if you do well, if you are successful, most people are envious and they covet your success and if you do poorly they revel in your misfortune and tell their friends that you have finally been humbled by the stock market—and that "*You had it coming*" for your reckless behavior. So silence is the best option since there is nothing to gain through informing people of your activities. The self-satisfaction for me is "BEING CORRECT" understanding and beating the tape

"On October 5, 1923, in order to practice my new techniques and theories, I moved my offices from 111 Broadway, uptown to 780 Fifth Avenue, the Heckscher Building. I designed the offices very carefully. I wanted to be away from the Wall Street atmosphere, out of earshot of any tips. I also wanted to gain more secrecy in my operations and more security, so that no one would know my trades. Sometimes I used over fifty brokers to keep my trades secret.

"Inside the building, there was a private express elevator that traveled only to my floor in the Penthouse. My offices occupied the entire penthouse floor. I purposely had no sign on the office door where the elevator stopped. Once inside, there was a small anteroom, a kind of waiting room where Harry Edgar Dache' had his desk.

"Harry was described by the New York press as 'Pug-ugly with a personality to match.' He stood a solid six feet six inches and weighed close to three hundred pounds with the battle-scarred face of a pugilist. Harry's looks belied his high intelligence. I interviewed him for only half an hour and hired him right on the spot. Harry had been in the Merchant Marine and traveled the globe many times. He spoke six languages, including Latin. He was a voracious reader, knowledgeable in many areas and a terrific administrator. He ran the office with secrecy and perfection. He was completely loyal to me and very protective of me and my family. The boys loved Harry. Jesse Jr. and Paul were enthralled with his magical stories of traveling the seven seas. He was their unofficial tutor, chauffeur, companion and bodyguard, especially when we went to Palm Beach.

"There were no windows in the ante-room, only a few chairs and Harry's desk. Behind Harry was the solid floor to ceiling door to my offices. There were no signs or identification on any doors. To let someone in to see me, Harry would first always confirm the appointment with me by intercom, no matter who it was. He would then rise from his desk and use his key to open the door for the visitor. It was a theatrical ritual that Harry performed to show the visitor the difficulty in gaining entrance into my 'Trading Room,' and it worked.

"Behind the door was a massive open room with a green chalk board that ran the entire length of the room. There was a catwalk in front of the chalkboard where four to six men would work in silence. They each would have a section of the "board" and they were responsible for specific stocks, active stocks or commodities that I was trading or observing closely.

"These men were paid very well and sworn to secrecy and Harry Dache' assured they remained loyal to me. Each man had on headphones that connected to the floor of the exchange. Men on the floor would call up the "instant" quotes to my board men, who would immediately write down the individual stock transaction—the bid, asked, and sold price. They did not work off the ticker tape. It was too slow. This gave me an edge on the ticker tape, which was usually delayed at least fifteen minutes and up to hours. I wanted the most current information I could get. I had learned as a young man how important "fresh" quotes were.

"If I was active in several stocks or commodities I would often increase my staff from four to six men on the "stock board." These men would work all day on the catwalk, in silence, only taking a short break for lunch, when they would usually be replaced by Harry, so no quotes were lost.

"These board men would always track two or more stocks in the same group. If I was trading General Motors, I would track, Ford or Chrysler as well, to observe the group action.

"In the middle of the office was a massive conference table of shiny mahogany with eight comfortable leather office armchairs. On the rare occasions when I had guests to my office I would always sit facing the chalkboard so I could watch the quotes as I listened to my guests. I often interrupted the meeting to enter my office and place trades in private.

"My private office was very large with heavy paneling of oak and mahogany. I had seen the paneling in a library in an old English manor and had purchased it. The library was disassembled and shipped to New York.

"My desk was large, made out of highly polished mahogany. On my desk was an "IN" basket and an "OUT" basket, a pad and pencil, nothing else. The adjacent wall to the mahogany desk that faced the "stock board" was a solid sheet of clear plate-glass, so I could see the market action as it happened from my desk.

"There were three black telephones on my desk. One was a direct wire to London, the second went to Paris and the third went directly to the floor of the Chicago grain pits. I wanted first hand, fresh information, and I was willing to pay for it. I knew that wars were won on information, intelligence, and the general with the best information, the best intelligence, was the general most likely to win. And I wanted no "rumors of war" I wanted only specific accurate information.

"Paul, my son, would often come to this office as he grew up, especially on his summer breaks. I would sometimes allow him to work the board. The board men were trained to work with a code. If a stock suddenly had a deep price fluctuations they would use a "secret code" to note this on the board. These codes were known only to the board men and myself. On occasion, there would be guests in the office who would ask me: J.L. what the hell are those weird columns on the chalkboard, some kind of hieroglyphics?"

"They make perfect sense to me." I would respond.

"You wanna explain them to me?"

"No." I would smile. "If I did, then you would be as smart as I am."

"Just tell me what to buy and sell—and when—keep it simple for me."

"You know I never recommend a stock, but I would be glad to tell you whether I believe the market is going up or down."

"It always goes up or down, J.L."

"You're right of course, but the trick is 'when' is it going to go up or down."

"And 'what's' going to go up or down, J.L. Don't forget it's 'what' particular stocks are going to go up or down; that's what we all want to know—what stock will rise and when."

"If a man knows the general trend of the market he should be able to do well."

"Whatever you say, J.L., whatever you say."

"One day I was sitting in my office talking to my son Paul. 'Turn around Paul, and look at the stock board.' Paul turned and studied the men as they moved on the catwalk like well-choreographed dancers.

"I continued: You see, son, those markings on that board are as clear to me as a musical score is to a great conductor. I see these symbols as alive, a rhythm, a heartbeat, a pulse, that makes beautiful music—it all makes perfect sense to me.

"For me the board is alive, like music, we are able to communicate. It's something that has come to me only after years of hard work and practice, not unlike a great conductor, of a great orchestra. What I feel when I look at that board, can't be shared, anymore than a conductor could articulate what he feels when he plays Mozart just the way it should be played. The board and those men are a playing a symphony to me, a symphony of money—that sings to me—that makes love to me—that envelops me in it's song."

Paul studied his father that afternoon. He believed every word. It was a rare moment for Paul, to get so intimate with his father who was a private man, stingy with his emotions, frugal with his love.

"I believe my job is to continually observe the tape and to interpret the tape as a person would look at a movie with no two frames exactly the same. These individual messages must be extracted from the tape and run through your brain in a rapid fashion. I carefully observe the market swings from five to twenty points that take from five to twenty working days. I also observe intensely the 3 and 6 point advances and declines...for all these factors play their part in forming the overall action on the stock market.

"I believe that the stock market always follows the line of least resistance until it meets with an at-first almost imperceptible force that slowly, but inexorably, stops its upward or downward movement. It is at these key junctures—the pivotal points—that the real money is made.

"I refer to them as pivotal points...these points are often difficult for the untrained "trader" to observe while they are happening. They become obvious at a later date when they have totally formed and the market has clearly changed direction. It is the job of the skillful stock trader to recognize and act in conjunction with these pivotal points and take his positions at the perfect psychological point, often these will involve industry groups falling out of favor and new groups rising and coming into favor.

"The savvy stock market trader controls his emotions and always acts in the future, not the present, and certainly never from the past. Therefore, like a crystal ball, the person who knows how to read the tape at these moments always seems to be able to identify these rising Industry Groups who will become the new strong sector-stocks for the new rally.

"People have always thought I was a "Bear Raider" who acted impulsively. Nothing could be further from the truth I have always been highly interested in the small and intermediate swings, as well as the longer trends. In fact, I'm interested in all movements of any kind that appear to me on the tape. I always considered it a personal challenge to try and figure out what the tape was saying. I knew what the great detective Sherlock Holmes knew, the clues are lying there in front of you, through calm deductive reasoning you must figure out the answer to the puzzle, discern what is lying there before you—many try but few succeed—"poise" "patience" and "silence" are the emotional keywords for the top trader.

"Just as the panics have always encouraged me to go long when things look the bleakest—conversely, when everything looks perfect and blissful it occurs to me that it may be time to go short. I try and see this before everyone else sees it, that is why I keep my own council in silence and avoid talking to anyone who may alter my thinking.

"Sometimes I have accumulated my line of stocks at what I believe to be the turning point in a great decline or at the crest of a mighty upward wave and I have carried this line for many months, even up to a year before I was proved correct. Because I understood that it requires time for general business to recover and for the earning power of these stocks to be reinstated so one must be patient and prudent in assembling their line of stocks for either a new rally or in going short in a downward trading market.

"I started trading at age 15 in the stock market; it has been the focus of my life. I was very fortunate in calling the crash of 1907 almost to the actual hour and very flattered when J.P. Morgan sent a special envoy to ask me to discontinue my short selling, which I did.

"On my best day during that decline of 1907 I made three million dollars in a single day. I was also fortunate in the depression of 1921 when I decided to go long with the market at its very lowest stages.

"And finally in the great depression of 1929 I went to the short side too early with the *"motors"* as they rolled over and I began my shorting—I lost over a quarter of a million dollars before I finally found the correct Reversal Pivotal Points for the rest of the leaders as they rolled over and tumbled headlong into the great depression. I went short in earnest at that moment and increased all my positions. I made the largest amount of money I had ever made during the market crash of 1929. I was even blamed personally by the press and the public for the crash, which was pure nonsense, nobody, no single person could cause a market to do something that it did not want to do.

"But please remember that I had been trading almost 40 years and I had a finely developed intuition as a result of the enormous experience I had attained. But I must say now in retrospect that in all these cases the clues were evident and spoke to meet as clearly as can be imagined. Volume was very important to me. I was a careful student in watching the way the selling was absorbed and the resistance, which it met from day-to-day. The volume of trades was always of key interest to me. I got this volume number from the ticker tape. There are people who believed I paid no attention to volume, some believed this because they came to my office and did not see the notations for volume. I kept the volume numbers often in my head or I just checked it at the end of the day's trading and had Harry, my office manager, post this final volume number in the master book on a stock I was particularly interested in.

"To me the people who invest in the market are akin to a large school of bait fish who have no specific leader, and they are capable of very quick, random-action whenever they fear they are in danger. In other words, there are millions of minds involved in the stock market, these minds form decisions based on the two main emotions in the stock market hope and fear—hope is often generated by greed—fear is often generated by ignorance.

"What this has always meant to me is that the key factor that drives the stock market is not intelligent analysis or reason...no, it is human emotions. Once a person understands this he will be a long way closer to becoming a successful stock market trader. With this in mind, a stock trader always has to look behind what he is seeing, with a careful analysis, remember everyone is basically receiving the same information, some win and some lose, based on how they interpret the information they receive.

"I have found that the ability to find the main turning points, the Reversal Pivotal Points, in the long trends is the most crucial and important thing a stock trader must do. I also believe that if all I could do during the panics and the booms was accurately find the perfect psychological moment to EXIT and ENTER the market I could amass a fortune of great proportion, for a successful trader must find and trade in the direction of the momentum—the direction of the line of least resistance. I have never had a problem in playing either side of the market because it was only logical to me to go long and to also go short. The market goes up a third of the time, down a third, and sideways a third of the time.

"If I am exiting a long position because I believe the stock has topped out, it is easy for me to get on the short side of that stock. I have no feeling for a stock as some people do. For instance, if I have made money with General Motors on the long side I have no feelings for General Motors—the stock has simply done what I had felt it would do. If I can now make a profit as General Motors declines—by going short—I will do so with no feeling toward the stock, which is after all an inanimate thing with no feelings for me. There are no good stocks nor are there any bad stocks; there are only stocks that make money for the speculator.

"I have heard many of my contemporaries say: 'That stock was good to me.' Or 'That stock cost me money, so I am staying away from it!' The stock had nothing to do with it. Everything that happens is a result of the Trader's judgment and 'no excuses' are acceptable. To put it simply it was the 'Trader' or 'Speculator' that made the conscious decision to enter a trade and always makes the conscious decision to exit a trade. The judgment was either correct or it wasn't.

"What all Traders must beware of is in effect a kind of arrogance, for when a stock moves against us we must decide that we were 'wrong' and we must exit that trade instantly. Most traders forget that it is a proven fact that we will always be wrong on some trades; it is getting out of those trades quickly that is the key to success.

"Another trap the inexperienced trader must deal with is trying to find the exact bottom and top of a major trading cycle. Remember, there are times when a trader must be out of the market and waiting on the sidelines. It is my experience that it is virtually impossible to call the exact top and the bottom of a market, but it is much better to err on the side of caution. Getting out and waiting for the market to establish itself is very difficult while you are invested, because by being invested you will have an automatic bias toward the direction of your position. If you are long you will subconsciously favor the longside, if you are short you will subconsciously favor the downside. Hope lives in us all, remember it is human nature to be hopeful. That is why I often sold out all my positions and re-evaluated the market from a cash position. It cost me the commissions, but for me I viewed this as a small insurance premium cost toward my overall goal. I also was well aware that all stocks do not top out at the same time, but stocks in industry groups often top out at the same time, as new groups move in to take their place. It is the overall trend of the leading groups that I watch.

"I have observed that the principle power of a bull market is purely money, the availability of money, and the real attitudes and emotions of men and women and whether these people are inclined to buy or sell stocks—I have always tracked the money flow as well as I could.

"I have further observed that is not what the millions of people think about the market, or say about the market...no, no, no, it is what they "*DO*" about the market by their actual buying and selling and all this is immediately revealed in the tape, the problem is in the interpretation of this news, this displayed evidence as the tape flows past the reader.

"This was my business, my life's vocation and the thing I most enjoyed. The work of solving the puzzle was what always fascinated me. It was never the money it was solving the puzzle, the money was the reward for solving the puzzle. Going broke, which happened to me several times in my life was the penalty for not solving the puzzle. The chief deception is that trading the market looks easy when it is one of the most difficult things to do—anticipate the trend. And the reason it is so difficult is because of human nature, controlling and conquering our human nature is the most difficult task. As I told my sons on many occasions: I lost money when I broke my own rules but when I followed the rules, I made money."

## How To Deal With Media Releases

"I have always been suspicious of everything I read in the newspaper and I never accept what I read at face value I try to look for hidden agendas and self-serving reasons that could have generated the articles, no matter what paper published the information. I understand that the market is composed of the reflections of the attitudes in the minds of millions and millions of people. But I try to read between the lines and formulate my own judgment; that is why I like to be alone to use my own judgment in situations such as reading the newspapers.

"Often people use the media to promote their stock and to influence public opinion to persuade the public and the pools into buying or selling, this is particularly true of large stock owners, pools and insiders. I interpret these newspaper articles in two ways:

"First, I try to interpret their immediate and direct influence on the opinions and actions of stock traders with regard to a particular stock.

"Second, I watch the actual stock quotes to detect how the news has influenced the buying and selling of specific stocks as a whole in that market industry group. Often my interpretation of a news event is wrong. But I always know that if the news-development is of sufficient importance it will eventually affect the tape.

"In other words, I watch the tape like a hawk to see how it is reacting to actual news. I do not listen to people, "the pundits," "the reporters" who are trying to interpret the news item and predict what will happen.

It is my experience that it is far better to look objectively at the tape, for the tape will provide the actual facts as to how the public is reacting to the news, these actual facts revealed by the tape are a far better indicator than any "reporter" or "pundit" can provide. It is up to the skillful market trader to watch the tape and react only to what the tape is saying. Learn how to read the tape—the truth is in the tape—listen to it.

## CUT YOUR LOSSES LET THE WINNERS RIDE
*Note: This conversation and story is excerpted from The Amazing Life of Jesse Livermore—World's Greatest Stock Broker written by Richard Smitten. The conversation between Jesse Livermore, Walter Chrysler (Chrysler Motors), Ed Kelley (head of United Fruit Co.) and T. Coleman Dupont (Dupont Family) and Colonel Ed Bradley in Bradley's Casino in Palm Beach–the longest running illegal gambling club in the United States.*

"I've been hearing rumors on the Street about you and a wheat trade. Tell us about it, J.L., entertain us at lunch."

"Well I just felt the demand for wheat in America was under estimated, and the price was going to rise. I waited for what I call my Pivotal Point and stepped in and bought 5 million bushels of wheat, about 7 million dollars worth.

"I watched the market closely after the purchase. It lagged. It was a dull market, but it never declined below where I bought it. Then one morning the market started upwards and after a few days the rise consolidated, forming another of my Pivotal Points. It laid around in there for a little while and then one day it popped out on the upside with heavy volume.

"A good signal, so I put in an order for another 5 million bushels. This order was filled at higher and higher prices. This was good news to me because it clearly indicated that the market line of least resistance was upwards.

"I liked the fact that it was much more difficult to acquire the second lot of 5 million bushels. I then had filled out my pre-determined target position of 10 million bushels, so I stepped back, and kept my eye on the market. It formed into a strong bull market and rose steadily for several months.

"When wheat rose 25 cents above my average price I cashed in. This was a bad mistake." Livermore paused as the lobster salads were served, and the second bottle of champagne was opened.

Walter Chrysler said, "J. L., how the hell could it be a bad mistake to make a profit of two and a half million dollars?"

"Because Walter, I sat back and watched wheat rise another 20 cents in price in three days."

"I still don't get it." Chrysler said.

"Why was I afraid? There was no good reason to sell the wheat. I simply wanted to take my profit."

"It still looks like a pretty good trade to me. I'm afraid you lost me, J.L." Ed Kelley added.

"All right, let me explain. You remember that old joke about the guy who goes to the race track and bets on the daily double and wins, then takes all his winnings and bets it on the third race and wins.

He does the same on all the other races, and wins. Then on the eighth and final race he takes his hundred thousand dollars in winnings and bets it all to win on a horse, and the horse loses."

"Yeah." Chrysler nodded.

"Well, he's walking out of the track and he meets a pal of his, who says. 'How'd you do today?'

"'Not bad,' he answers, smiling, 'I lost two bucks.'"

They laughed. "That's a good story J.L., but how the hell does it apply to the wheat story?" Chrysler asked.

"Simple, why was I afraid of losing the track's money, my profits, in effect. I was simply acting out of fear. I was in too big a hurry to convert a paper profit into a cash profit. I had no other reason for selling out that wheat, except that I was afraid to lose the profit I had made."

"What's wrong with being afraid?" Dupont asked.

"So, what did you do, J.L.?" Kelley asked.

"Well, after I booked my profit in the wheat I realized I had made a great mistake. I had not had the courage to play the deal out to the end—'till I got a signal to sell, a real definitive sell signal."

"So..."

"I re-entered the market and went back at an average price 25 cents higher than where I had sold out my original position. It rose another 30 cents, and then it gave a danger signal, a real strong danger signal. I sold out near the high of $2.06 a bushel. About a week later it sold off to $1.77 a bushel."

"Well, you have more guts than me, J.L., and it sounds a little like greed to me."

"That's because you sell fruit, Ed. The way you know how to

diagnose the market on fruit is the way I am supposed to know how to diagnose the stock and commodities markets, and the wheat futures market had shown no signs of weakness when I first sold it.

"The next time I sold the wheat it was different, I could see definite symptoms of weakness. It gave the clues, the hints, the tell tale signs of topping out. The tape always gives plenty of warning time for the savvy speculator to heed."

"Well, J.L., I like your story but sometimes I think maybe you got a set of those lucky horseshoes up your ass, just like Ed Bradley here." Chrysler added.

"Well Walter, a little luck never hurt anyone." Livermore paused and looked around at the group. "I'd say we all had our share of luck at one time or another."

They all laughed.

## THE WILL

Livermore agreed with his friend, the gambler, Colonel Ed Bradley—after TIMING and MONEY MANAGEMENT comes EMOTIONS...it is one thing to know what to do. It is quite another thing to have the will to actually do it. This is true of the stock market. This is true of life. Who knew better than Jesse Livermore. He explained to his sons:

"I believe that having the discipline to follow your rules is essential. Without specific, clear, and tested rules speculators do not have any real chance of success. Why, because speculators without a plan are like a general without a strategy, and therefore without an actionable battle plan. Speculators without a single clear plan can only act and react, act and react, to the 'slings and arrows of stock market misfortune,' until finally they are defeated.

"It is my conclusion that playing the market is partly an art form, it is not just pure reason. If it were pure reason, then somebody would have figured it out long ago. That's why I believe every speculator must analyze his own emotions to find out just what stress level he can endure. Every speculator is different, every human psyche is unique, every personality exclusive to an individual. Learn your own emotional limits before attempting to speculate, that is my advice to any one who has ever asked me what makes a successful speculator. If you can't sleep at night because of your stock market position than you have gone too far, if this is the case then sell your position down to the sleeping level.

"On the other hand, I believe anyone who is intelligent, conscientious and willing to put in the necessary time, can be successful on Wall Street. As long as they realize the market is a business like any other business—they have a good chance to prosper.

"I believe that behind all major movements in the stock market there are irresistible forces at work. This is all the successful speculator needs to know. Just be aware of the actual stock movements and act upon that knowledge. It is too difficult to match up world events or current events, or economic events with the movements of the stock market. This is true because the stock market always moves ahead of world events. The stock market is not operating in the present or reflecting the present; it is operating on what is yet to be the future. The market often moves contrary to apparent common sense and world events, as if it had a mind of its own, designed to fool most people, most of the time. Eventually the truth of why it moved as it did will emerge.

"It is therefore foolish to try and anticipate the movement of the market based on current economic news and current events, such as: The Purchasing Managers Report, the Balance of Payments, Consumer Price Index and the Unemployment figures, even the rumor of war, because these are already factored into the market. It is not that I ignored these facts or was ignorant of them, I wasn't. I was well aware of world events, political events, and economic events. But these facts were not facts I could ever use to "PREDICT" the market. After the market moved it would be 'rationalized' in endless post mortems by the financial pundits and later when the dust had settled, the real economic, political and world events would eventually be brought into focus by historians as to the actual reasons why the market acted as it had. But, by that time it was too late to make any money.

"Trying to figure out the 'why' of a market move can often cause great emotional strife. The simple fact is, the market always precedes economic news, it does not react to economic news. The market lives and operates in future time. Example: A good earnings statement is issued by a company and the stock proceeds to fall in price-why? Because the market had already factored in those earnings.

"One of the problems with looking too deeply into economic news is that it may plant 'suggestions' in your mind, and suggestions can be subliminal and dangerous to your emotional stock market health where you have to deal in reality. These suggestions are very often logical but that does not mean they are true and will effect the market.

"I have never understood why people think making money in the market is easy. We all have our own businesses. I would never ask my good friend Ed Kelley, the head of the United Fruit Company, to tell me the secrets of the fruit business, or Walter Chrysler about the automotive business. It would just never dawn on me. So, I could never understand when people asked me: How can I make some fast money in the stock market?

"I always smiled and said to myself—How could I possibly know how *YOU* could make money in the market? I always evaded the question. It was like asking me, how can I make some quick money in brain surgery? Or how can I make a few fast bucks defending some person in a murder case? I believe, from experience, that even attempting to answer these questions effects a person's emotions, because you have to take a firm position and defend your thoughts, which may change tomorrow, depending on the conditions of the market.

"But I fully understood that I was not the only one who knew that the stock market is the world's biggest gold mine, sitting at the foot of the island of Manhattan. A gold mine that opens its doors everyday and invites any and all people in to plumb its depths and leave with wheelbarrows full of gold bars, if they can, and I have done it. The gold mine is there all right, and I believe everyday someone plumbs its depths, and when the bell rings at the end of the day they have gone from pauper to prince, or from prince to supreme potentate...or stony broke. And it's always there, waiting.

"I believe that uncontrolled basic emotions are the true and deadly enemy of the speculator, hope, fear and greed are always present, sitting on the edge of our psyches, waiting on the sidelines, waiting to jump into the action, plow into the game.

"This is one of the reasons I never use the words 'Bullish' or 'Bearish.' These words are not in my vocabulary, because I believe these words can create an emotional mind-set of a specific market direction in a speculator's mind. The words Bull and Bear cause a trader to get a fixed mind-set. And there is a good chance the speculator will blindly follow that trend or direction for an extended period of time, even if the facts change.

"I have found that well-defined trends do not last for extended periods of time. When people ask me for a tip I say the market is currently in an 'Upward Trend' or a 'Downward Trend' or a 'Sideways Trend'—or I tell them that the 'line of least resistance' is currently up or down,' as the case may be...and that is all I say.

"This leaves me with the flexibility to change my mind, according to market behavior. I try never to 'PREDICT' or 'ANTICIPATE' the market. I only try to "REACT" to what the market is telling me by its behavior.

"I firmly believe that there are always clues as to what is going to come next. The clues are buried in the behavior of the market—what the market actually does—the here and now—not what is predicted that it will do. In a way, you have to be like a detective and solve the puzzle using the facts that you are given. But, like a good detective, always look for proof of your facts and re-confirm them if possible always get corroboration. This requires an unemotional analysis.

"And I am one of the few speculators who has never cared in which direction a stock is going. I simply go with the 'line of least resistance.' For me it is simply 'a market play,' the direction of the stock is not important. In fact, one of the reasons I was noted as 'The Great Bear of Wall Street' was that so few other speculators had the courage of their convictions to play the downside, the negative side of the market.

"When stocks decline swiftly, and abruptly, they are being driven by fear. When they rise they are being driven by hope. If people are hoping a stock will rise they are slower to sell. If they fear the stock will decline they are usually fast to dump that stock. That is why declines produce faster, more abrupt market action. So, if you play the short side you must react to faster, more drastic market patterns and conditions.

"There is no good direction to trade, short or long, there is only the 'money making' way to trade. I have observed that to sell short goes against human nature, which is basically optimistic and positive. I believe less than 4% of speculators ever trade the short side of the stock market. There is also no question that it is *"extremely dangerously"* to sell short because the potential loss is unlimited. It takes strong control of your emotions to trade on the short side.

"But the stock market moves up roughly a third of the time, sideways a third of the time, and downward a third of the time. If you only played the bull-side of the market you were out of the action, and a chance to make money two thirds of the time. And for good or bad I was not a man who wanted to wait, and hope, and wonder. I wanted to trade the market, and I wanted to win more times than I lost.

"I am fully aware that of the millions of people who speculate in the stock market few people spend full time involved in the art of speculation. Yet, as far as I am concerned it is a full-time job, perhaps even more than a job, perhaps it is a vocation—where many are called and few are singled out for success.

## BEWARE OF STOCK TIPS

"By far, the hardest emotional battle a speculator must deal with is tips. It was the main reason I moved uptown to Fifth Avenue, to get out of the reach of everyone who was trying to help me by giving me 'sure things' and 'inside information.' Beware of all 'inside information' and 'tips.'

"Tips come from all sources. Once, long ago, one of these tips was passed on to me from the Chairman of a major American corporation who spoke to me at a dinner party at my house in Great Neck.

"How are things going?" I asked him.

"Great, we've turned the company around, not that it was really in trouble, but it looks like clear sailing from here. In fact, our quarterly earnings are coming out in a week and they are going to be terrific."

"I liked him and believed him. So, the next morning I bought a thousand shares to test it out. The earnings came in just as the chief executive said they would. The stock rose nicely, the earnings continued to rise for the next three quarters, and the stock rose steadily. I was lulled into a feeling of security, as the stock continued to rise. Then it stopped and started plummeting in the opposite direction, like a waterfall.

"I called the Chairman and said: This fall in your stock price has me worried. What's going on?"

He answered. "I know the price has fallen J.L., but we consider it nothing more than a natural correction—after all we have had a pretty damn steady rise in the price of the stock for almost a year now."

"How's business?" I asked.

"Well, our sales are slightly off and that news may have leaked out, I'm afraid. Looks like the "bears" got hold of that information and are hammering the stock. It's mostly short selling, a bear raid, we think. We'll drive them out on the next rally, squeeze them a little, eh J.L.?"

"Are you guys selling any of your holdings?" I asked.

"Absolutely not! Where would I put my money with more safety than my own company?"

"Well, sure enough, I later found out that the *'insiders'* were busy selling into the stock's strength, the minute they got wind of the business going into a slump.

"I never got mad. It was my stupidity and greed. I knew that all key executives were basically cheerleaders and they must remain positive, must be bearers of only good news. They could never tell shareholders or competitors that things were not as "rosy" as they appeared. In fact, it always made me smile to listen to their mendacity. The misstatements, the lies, were just a matter of 'self-preservation,' an essential part of the job of a chief executive officer—at every level of power, including politics.

"But it was my self-preservation I was interested in, not the top executives and shareholders of the companies I invested in. Therefore after a while, and some substantial lost money, I never asked an insider about how their business was doing.

"Why waste my time listening to half-truths, shadowy statements, inaccurate projections, and just plain bold-faced lies when I could simply just look at the behavior of the stock. The story was clear in the action of the stock. The truth was in the tape for anyone and everyone to see.

" I have suggested to people who were interested in the stock market that they carry around a small notebook, keep notes on interesting general market information and perhaps develop their own stock market trading strategy. I always suggested, that the first thing they write down in their little notebooks was:

## "BEWARE OF INSIDE INFORMATION...ALL INSIDE INFORMATION!"

"There is only one way to achieve success in speculation—through hard work, persistently hard work. If there is any easy money lying around no one is going to try and give it to me—this I know. My satisfaction always came from beating the market, solving the puzzle. The money was the reward, but it was not the main reason I loved the market. The stock market is the greatest, most complex puzzle ever invented, and it pays the biggest jackpot.

"And always remember: You can win a horse race, but you can't beat the races. You can win on a stock, but you cannot beat Wall Street all the time—nobody can.

"People always talked about my instincts, especially after the Union Pacific story and the San Francisco earthquake. But I never thought my instincts were that special. The instincts of a seasoned speculator are really no different than the instincts of a farmer, like my father. In fact, I consider farmers the biggest gamblers in the world. Planting their crops every year, gambling on the price of wheat, corn, or cotton, or soybeans, choosing the right crop to plant, gambling on the weather and insects—the unpredictable demand for the crop—what was more speculative. These same principles apply to all business. So, after twenty, thirty, forty years, of growing wheat or corn or raising cattle or making automobiles or bicycles, the person naturally gets his sixth sense, his intuition, his experienced-based-hunches for his business. I consider myself no different.

"The only area I may have differed from most speculators, was when I felt I was truly right, dead right, for-damn-sure right—then I would go all the way, shoot the works. The way I did during the 1929 market crash when I had a line of one million shares of stock out on the short side, and every rise and fall of a single point meant a million dollars to me. Even then, my biggest play, it was never the money that drove me. It was the game, solving the puzzle, beating a game that confused and confounded the greatest minds in the history of mankind. For me, the passion, the challenge, the exhilaration, was in beating the game, a game that was a living dynamic riddle, a conundrum, to all the men and women who speculated on Wall Street.

"Perhaps it was like combat is to a soldier. It's a mental high that's visceral, where all your senses are pushed to the limit and the stakes are very high.

"I told my boys—stay in the business your good at, and I was good at speculating. Over the years I took *"many millions"* of dollars out of Wall Street and invested them in Florida land, aircraft companies, oil wells, and new "miracle" products based on new inventions—they were all abject failures, disasters. I lost every cent I ever invested in them.

"Just remember, without discipline, a clear strategy, and a concise plan the speculator will fall into all the emotional pitfalls of the market and jump from one stock to another, hold a losing position too long, cut-out of a winner too soon, and for no reason other than fear of losing the profit. Greed, fear, impatience, ignorance and hope, will all fight for mental dominance over the speculator. Then, after a few failures and catastrophes the speculator may become demoralized, depressed, despondent, and abandon the market and the chance to make a fortune from what the market has to offer.

"Develop your own strategy, discipline and approach to the market. I offer my suggestions as one who has traveled the road before you. Perhaps I can act as a guide for you and save you from falling into some of the pitfalls that befell me.

"But in the end the decisions must be your own."

## Chapter 11

# TRADE LIKE JESSE LIVERMORE
## In The New Millennium

### Using the Computer — Trading System Preview

The Jesse Livermore method of market trading will soon be available on a computer system that will be tied into a live stock market feed. This feed supplies a 15 minute-behind-real-time database. This Livermore system will provide a two-fold basis to trade like "Livermore." The first option will be to enter a virtual stock market world where everything will be real except the trader will use virtual money. The participant will receive a stake of 100,000 dollars in "virtual money." Livermore believed "if you don't put your money on the table you can never test your judgment." The second option will allow the participant to trade the stock market using real money.

This chapter is a small preview of how the software program will perform.

Jesse Livermore never used charts. He used mathematical analysis to draw his conclusions. There is no doubt that Jesse Livermore would have taken advantage of every single technology and modern method to increase the volume and accuracy of information that was available to him. It would only be logical for him to use graphic analysis as well as his mathematical theories. There is no doubt that this graphic analysis would have included charts.

151

As a result, to help explain his basic fundamental approach to the market, graphic tools will be used.

**$ TDT—TOP DOWN TRADING** — The concept of "Top Down Trading" is very straightforward, before making a trade on any particular stock you must first check off the following items, like a pilot checks off the pre-flight list.

**$ TM — THE MARKET** — Check the line of least resistance for the overall current market direction. Remember, Livermore never used the terms "Bull" or "Bear" because they forced a mind-set that he believed made the mind less flexible. He used the term *"Line of least resistance."* He checked to be sure the current line of least resistance was positive, negative or neutral—sideways. Be sure to check the exact market the stock trades in for instance: Dow, NASDAQ, or Amex—before executing the trade. It is essential to make sure the lines of least resistance are in the direction of your trade before entering the trade.

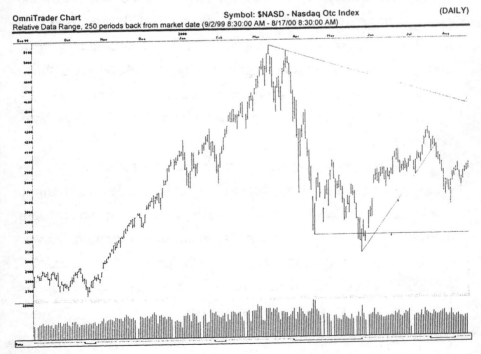

OmniTrader Chart      Symbol: $NASD - Nasdaq Otc Index     (DAILY)
Relative Data Range, 250 periods back from market date (9/2/99 8:30:00 AM - 8/17/00 8:30:00 AM)

**$ TIG — THE INDUSTRY GROUP** — Check the specific industry group. For instance, if you are considering a trade in ATT check out the Telecommunication Long Distance Group. If you are looking at a trade in Haliburton, check out the Oil Well Drilling group. If you are looking at a trade in Harrah Entertainment check out the Gambling Group, make sure the group is moving in the correct direction, the line of least resistance to provide a profit for you on the trade you have selected.

## INTERNET GROUP

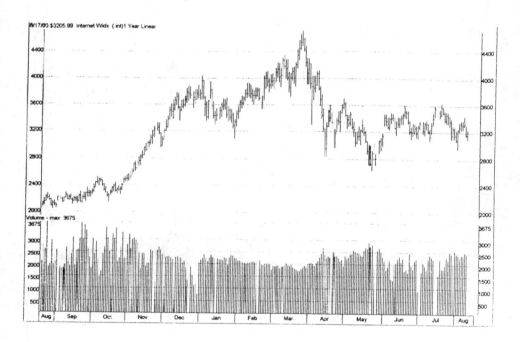

**$ TT — TANDEM TRADING —** Check the stock and the Sister Stock and compare them. If you are going to trade in General Motors check a Sister Stock like Ford or Chrysler. If you are going to trade Best Buy than check out Circuit City—a Sister Stock. Tandem Trading requires the trader to place two stocks of the same group next to each other.

**YAHOO**                                    **AMERICA ON LINE**

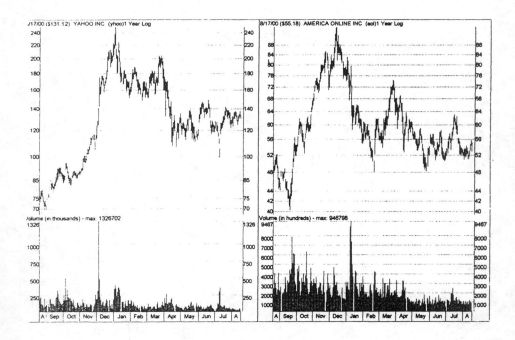

4–Do a final thorough analysis of the individual stock you have decided to trade. This is your responsibility, your obligatory "Due Diligence." This final step would be similar to traveling down the runway–but not lift off— a final chance to change your mind before you "pull the trigger" and buy the stock. This final step must be completed by you, and you alone...make this decision on your own–it's your money.

TOP DOWN TRADING–summary chart

**$ TDT —Below: NASDAQ, Internet, Yahoo, America on Line**

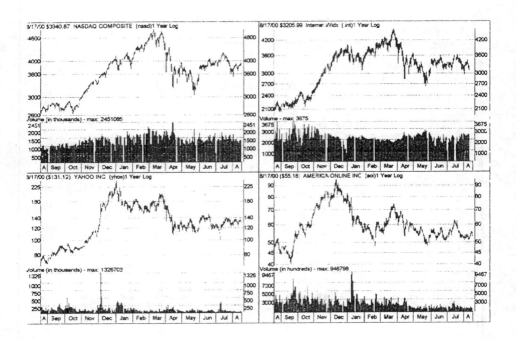

## COMMON CHART FORMATIONS
## THAT CONFIRM LIVERMORE TRADES

**$ RPP — PIVOT POINTS** — A Reversal Pivotal Point is described by Livermore as the perfect psychological moment to buy a stock–it is a reversal in trend. *"A CHANGE IN BASIC MARKET DIRECTION– THE PERFECT PSYCHOLOGICAL TIME AT THE BEGINNING OF A NEW MOVE, IT IS A MAJOR CHANGE IN THE BASIC TREND."*

7-15-99           SCHLUMBERGER LTD (SLB)           64.56

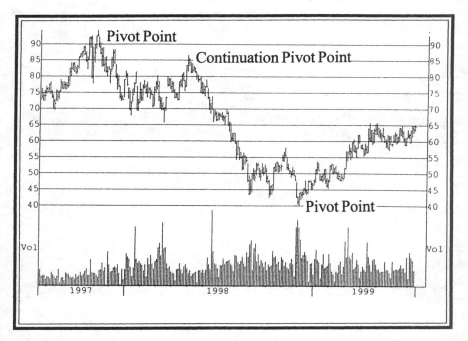

*SCHLUMBERGER formed a Continuation Pivotal Point in mid-1998 when it hit $86, confirming the descent, in this case, to $40 near the end of 1998.*

**$ CPP — Continuation Pivot Point** — A Continuation Pivot Point is confirmation that a move has corrected and remained in the same upward trend. This is a period of consolidation. It does two things:

—it confirms that the basic trend has not changed

— it provides a place to buy or to increase your existing position.

But remember, you should only increase your position after the stock has broken out on the upside.

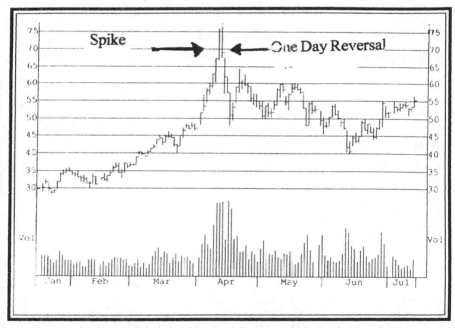

7-15-99          SCHWAB CHARLES CORP NEW (SCH)          55.37

*In this case Charles Schwab, a brokerage firm, had a dramatic rise of over 15 points in 3 days that developed into a spike. During the last day of the ascent the rally breaks down near the end of the day and the price of the stock falls and closes near the low of the day. The next morning it opens and falls further. These one-day reversals are often accompanied by increased volume. This scenario was a screaming "danger signal" to Livermore.*

**$ S — SPIKES** — A Spike is a series of dramatic rises at the end of a move—three successive days or more with a dramatic increase in the price of a stock accompanied by heavy volume–this is a warning and in all likely hood is not good news.

**$ DR — ONE DAY REVERSAL** — I define it as: "A One Day Reversal occurs where the high of the day is higher than the high of the previous day, but the close of the day is below the close of the previous day and the volume of the current day is higher than the volume of the previous day. Beware!"

**MAJOR DANGER SIGNAL**
**POSSIBLE TREND REVERSAL.**

7-15-99      GENERAL MOTORS CORPORATION (GM)      68.06

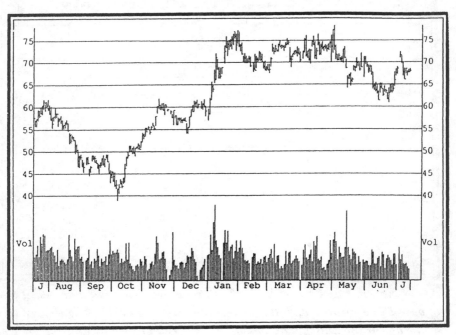

*From January until early May GM traded in a base between 70 and 75*

**$ BOCB–BREAKOUT FROM A CONSOLIDATING BASE** — A breakout from a consolidating base pattern on heavy volume is usually a signal of a coming move in the stock. The consolidating base patterns can take various forms.

**$ BONH** — **BREAKOUT ON A NEW HIGH** — Be alert for a breakout on high volume that establishes a clear new high on a stock. The logic for this was explained in the previous text–when a stock makes a new high it means that it has powered through the overhead supply. Many people buy a stock at its high and as it declines they will not sell, waiting instead for a rally to put the stock up to the point where they purchased the stock. They wait and wait and when the stock finally gets up into the area of the old high, a tremendous amount of distribution usually takes place as the shareholders sell their positions until finally the skies clear and the stock breaks through and climbs to a new high where there is no stock overhanging the market. This pattern also proves that the stock had enough interest and demand to clear up the old stockholders and climb higher.

7-15-99                    BEST BUY INC (BBY)                    76.18

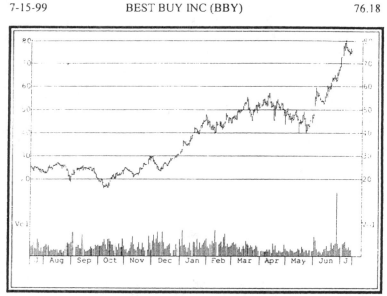

*Best Buy, a consumer retailer of electronics, appliances, and entertainment software, broke out of a long consolidation at $30 in December of 1998 and kept right on climbing to new highs.*

**$ BV — Big Volume** — Volume was a key indicator to Livermore as it should be to any successful trader. Volume represents the number of shares being traded in a particular Market (Dow, Nasdaq) or Industry Group, say telecommunications or a particular stock. It is simply an indicator of supply and demand. If the volume increases in an upwardly moving Market, Industry Group or Stock it means that there is accelerated interest in the situation and it is being accumulated. And conversely, if a stock is in a downward trend and it is hit by heavy volume it means that the stock is being sold and therefore distribution is occurring. The volume should be checked on both a daily basis and a weekly basis.

Livermore began to closely watch a stock if the volume increased fifty percent above the normal weekly volume. He could calculate this figure in his head. He had the daily closing volume numbers of the stock he was watching posted in a book by Harry Dache,' his office manager.

7-15-99     CAPITAL ONE FINANCIAL CORP (COF)     48.93

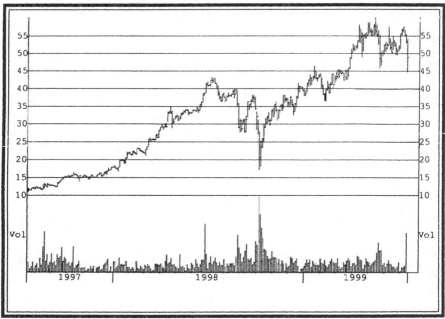

*Note Example: Capital One Financials' terrific volume, and spike down, in early October shows a clear "high-volume climax-bottom" that indicates the downward trend has changed. Be alert that VOLUME is often a key confirming signal to indicate a change in direction.*

# Chapter 12

# How To Trade in Stocks

## ADDENDUM—TRADING GUIDE

### LIVERMORE LAWS—TRADING SECRETS REVEALED

*"To Know is to do!"—Socrates—*

A successful speculator remains a constant student of THREE THINGS:

MARKET TIMING—When to enter and when to exit a market trade—"when to hold 'em when to fold 'em," as Livermore's friend and Palm Beach Casino owner Ed Bradley used to say.

MONEY MANAGEMENT—Don't lose money—don't lose your stake, your line. A speculator without cash is like a store owner with no inventory. Cash is a speculator's inventory, his lifeline, his best friend—without it you're out of business. Don't lose your line!

EMOTIONAL CONTROL—Before you can successfully play the market you must have a clear concise strategy and stick to it. Every speculator must design an intelligent battle plan, customized to suit their emotional makeup, before speculating in the stock market. The biggest thing a speculator has to control is his emotions. Remember, the stock market is not driven by reason, logic, or pure economics. It is driven by human nature which never changes. How can it change, it's our nature.

## "YOU CAN'T TELL IF YOUR JUDGMENT IS RIGHT UNTIL YOU PUT YOUR MONEY ON THE LINE"

Livermore: "If you don't put your money on the table you can never test your judgment, because you can never test your emotions. And I believe it is emotion, not reason that dictates the direction of the stock market, just like most important things in life: love, marriage, children, war, sex, crime, passion, religion. It is rarely reason that drives people.

"This is not to say things like sales, profits, world conditions, politics, and technology do not play a part in the ultimate price of a stock. These factors eventually come to bear, and the price of the stock market and the individual stocks may reflect these factors, but it is always emotion that carries the extremes.

"I believe in cycles, in life cycles and market cycles. They are often extreme, hardly ever balanced. Cycles come like a series of ocean waves, bringing the high tide when things are good, and as conditions recede, the low tide appears. These cycles come unexpectedly, unpredictably, and they have to be weathered with temperance, poise and patience—good or bad. But remember, the skillful speculator knows that money can be made no matter what the market conditions, if a speculator is willing to play both sides of the market, as I was."

## 5 Year Chart of the NASDAQ

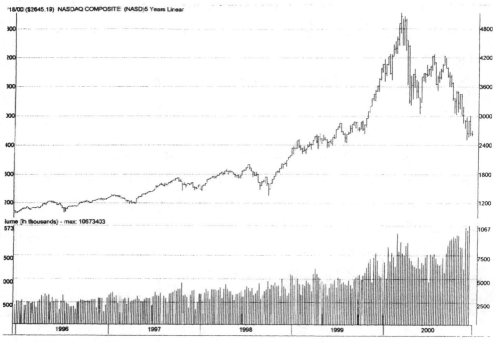

## MARKET RULES

"I long ago realized that the stock market is never obvious. It is designed to fool most of the people, most of the time. My rules are often based on thinking against the grain, against human nature:

* Cut your losses quickly;

* Be sure to confirm your judgment before you take your full position;

* Let your profits ride if there is no good reason to close out the position;

* The action is with the leading stocks, these can change with every new market;

* Keep the number of stocks you follow limited in order to focus;

* New all time highs are possible signals of valid break outs;

*Cheap stocks often appear to be bargains after a large drop. They often continue to fall, or have little potential to rise in price. Leave them alone!

* Use Pivotal Points to identify trend changes and confirmations in trends;

* Don't fight the tape!

"The stock market is a study in cycles, when it changes direction it remains in that new trend until the momentum weakens–a body in motion tends to stay in motion –remember don't buck the trend– don't fight the tape.

"In a free market system–PRICES FLUCTUATE! They never go up all the time, and they never go down all the time. This is good for the alert speculator, since either side of the market can be played."

## TIMING RULES

*The big money is made by 'the sitting and the waitin'—not the thinking. Wait until all the factors are in your favor before making a trade—follow the Top Down Trading rules. Once a position is taken the next difficult task is to be patient and wait for the move to play out. The temptation is strong to take fast profits or cover your trade solely out of fear of losing the profit on a correction. This error has cost millions of speculators millions of dollars. Be sure you have a good clear reason to enter a trade and be sure you have good clear reasons to exit your position. It is the big swing that makes the big money for you.

*Play the market only when all factors are in your favor. No person can play the market all the time and win. There are times when you should be completely out of the market.

*The only thing to do when a person is wrong is to be right, by ceasing to be wrong. Cover your losses quickly, without hesitation. Don't waste time, when a stock moves below a mental-stop, sell it immediately.

*Stocks often act like human beings, expressing different personalities: aggressive, reserved, hyper-high-strung, direct, logical, predictable, unpredictable. Study the stocks like you would study people, after a while their reactions to certain circumstances become predictable, and useful, in timing the stock's movement.

*Stocks are never too high to begin buying or too low to begin selling short.

*Failure to take the opportunity to get out of large illiquid positions when the opportunity presents itself can cost.

*Failure to take advantage of a serendipitous act of good luck in the stock market is often a mistake.

*In a market moving sideways in a narrow channel where stock prices are essentially stagnant, there is a great danger in trying to predict or anticipate WHEN, and in what DIRECTION the market will move. You must wait until the market or the stock breaks out of this sideways channel in either direction. DON'T ANTICIPATE! Wait for market confirmation! Never argue with the tape. Follow the line of least resistance. Follow the evidence.

* Do not spend a lot of time trying to figure out what moves the price of a particular stock. Rather, examine the tape. The answer always lies in *"WHAT"* the tape says, not trying to figure out the *"WHY."* Behind all major movements in the stock market there is an irresistible force, which will most likely be revealed later. That is all the successful speculator needs to know.

*The stock market goes up, down and sideways. You can make money on the up side or the down side—you can buy long or sell short. It should not matter to you what side of the market you are on. You must be impersonal. When the market goes sideways and you are confused, take a vacation.

*A danger signal: the *"ONE DAY REVERSAL,"* where the high of the day is higher than the high of the previous day, but the close of the day is below the close or the low of the previous day and the volume of the current day is higher than the volume of the previous day. Beware!

* If the stock you traded is going in the opposite direction than you expected-sell it quickly. It means your judgment was wrong—cut your losses quickly.

* Wait, be patient, until as many factors as possible are in your favor, before making a trade—it's the patience that makes the money.

* Study the action of a stock that has made a severe break in price, a precipitous drop. If the stock does not rebound quickly it will most likely fall away further—there is an inherent weakness in this stock, the reason will be revealed at a later time.

*The market is operating in future time. It has usually already factored in current events.

*It is the inception of a basic movement, the Pivotal Point, a change in trend, which indicates whether to buy or sell. It is this change in trend that, if caught, yields the most rewards.

*There are two kinds of Pivotal Points. The Reversal Pivotal Point, defined as the *"perfect psychological time at the beginning of a major market move, a change in basic trend."* It does not matter if it is at the bottom or top of a long-term trending move.

The second Pivotal Point is called the "Continuation Pivotal Point." The "Reversal Pivotal Point" marked a definite change in direction, the "Continuation Pivot Point" confirms the move is underway–it is a natural consolidation before the next move upward.

Be alert, major Pivotal Points can often be accompanied by a heavy increase in "VOLUME."

Pivotal Points are an essential TIMING device, a trigger that reveals when to enter, and when to exit the market.

* At the end of a bull market, watch for wild capitalizations, good stocks selling at 30, 40, 50, 60 times their annual earnings. These will be the same stocks that had normally traded at 8 to 12 times earnings.

* Beware of wild speculative stocks that take off for no real reasons, except that they are "trendy, in-favor stocks."

* "NEW HIGHS" are very important for timing. A new all-time high can mean that the stock has broken through the overhead supply of stock and the line of least resistance will be strongly upward. The majority of people, when they see that a stock has made a new high, sell it immediately, then look for a cheaper stock.

## TOP DOWN TRADING—FOLLOW THE
## TREND—CHECK THE MAIN MARKET

The speculator must know the overall trend of the market before making a trade—*THE LINE OF LEAST RESISTANCE*. Know if this line of *"least resistance"* is upward or downward. This applies to both the overall market and individual stocks. The basic thing you need to know before making a trade is which way the overall market is headed, up, down, or sideways. You have to decide this first before making a trade. If the overall trend of the market is not in your favor you are playing at an extreme disadvantage–Remember, go with the flow, bend with the trend, do not sail into a gale, and most of all...don't argue with the tape!

* GROUP ACTION IS A KEY TO TIMING—Stocks do not move alone when they move. If U.S. Steel climbs in price then sooner or later Bethlehem, Republic and Crucible will follow along. The premise is simple, if the basic reasons are sound why U.S. Steel's business should come into favor in the stock market, then the rest of the steel group should also follow for the same reasons.

*Trade the leading stocks in the leading groups. Buy the strongest market leader in an industry group.

* Watch the market leaders, the stocks that have led the charge upward in a bull market. When these stocks falter and fail to make new highs, it is often a signal that the market has turned. As the leaders go so goes the entire market.

* Confine your studies of stock market movements to the prominent issues of the day, the leaders. If you cannot make money out of the leading active issues, you are not going to make money out of the stock market. That is where the action is and where the money is to be made. It also keeps your universe of stocks limited, focused and more easily controlled.

*Before you buy a stock, you should have a clear target where to sell if the stock moves against you, a firm stop. And you must obey your rules!

*A successful market trader must only bet on the course of highest probabilities. Buy small positions, probe first, to test your judgement before you commit to a large position. Do not establish your full position all at one time—use probes to confirm your judgment and timing and to find the line of *"least resistance."* The *"probing approach"* is also a major factor in "Money Management."

*The trader must react quickly to the *"unexpectable,"* which is never predictable. If it is a windfall, grab it. If it is bad news, hit the road, and don't look back or hesitate—sell out the position.

*Beware after a long trend up when volume gets heavy, and stocks churn. This is a clue, a red-alert warning that the end of the move is near. This is also a possible indication of stocks going from strong hands to weak hands, from the professional to the public from accumulation to distribution. The public often views this heavy volume as the mark of a vibrant, healthy market going through a normal correction, not a top or a bottom.

## MONEY MANAGEMENT RULES

*ESTABLISH STOPS!—The speculator should have a clear target where to sell if the stock moves against you. This is essential on the first buys—trailing stops can also be used as the stock moves, although I always did these with trailing mental stops. And you must obey your rules! Never sustain a loss of more than ten percent of your invested capital. Losses can be twice as expensive to make up. This was learned in the bucket shops—working with 10% margin. You were automatically sold out by the bucket shops if the loss exceeded the 10% limit. The 10% loss rule is an important rule for managing money. As noted, this is also a key "timing" rule.

*NEVER SUSTAIN A LOSS OF MORE THAN 10%*
*OF INVESTED CAPITAL.*

IF YOU LOSE 50% YOU MUST GAIN 100% TO GET
EVEN—

LIVERMORE 10% LOSS TABLE

| STARTING POSITION | AMT LOST | REMAINDER | %LOSS | % TO RECOVER LOSS |
|---|---|---|---|---|
| $1000 | $80 | $920 | 8.0 | 8.7 |
| | 100 | 900 | 10.0 | 11.1 |
| | 200 | 800 | 20.0 | 25.0 |
| | 300 | 700 | 30.0 | 42.8 |
| | 400 | 600 | 40.0 | 66.6 |
| | 500 | 500 | 50.0 | 100.0 |

*Never meet a margin call and never average down in your buying.

*Turn paper profits into 'real money' periodically. Take a percent of your winnings and put them in a safe place, like the bank or bonds, or an annuity. Cash was, is, and always will be—king. Always have cash in reserve. Cash is the ammunition in your gun. My biggest mistake was not in following this rule more often.

*Examine and understand the dimension of time:

*"TIME IS NOT MONEY BECAUSE THERE MAY BE TIMES WHEN YOUR MONEY SHOULD BE INACTIVE—TIME IS TIME—*

*AND— MONEY IS MONEY—OFTEN MONEY THAT IS JUST SIT-TING CAN LATER BE MOVED INTO THE RIGHT SITUATION AND MAKE A FORTUNE–PATIENCE–PATIENCE–PATIENCE WAS THE KEY TO SUCCESS—DON'T BE IN A HURRY."*

*Don't be in a hurry. The successful investor is not invested in the market all the time—there are many times when you should be completely in cash. If you are unsure of the direction of the market then stay out and wait for a confirmation of the next move.

*Use "PROBES" to establish your full position. After an initial "PROBE" do not make a second move until the first "PROBE" shows you a profit. Do not establish your full position all at once, wait until your first trades, your early "PROBES," have shown you a profit, then go ahead and fill out your full position.

To be precise: First establish 20% of your planned position on the first purchase, 20% on the second, 20% on the third.

Wait for a confirmation of your judgment—then make your final purchase of 40%.

Consider each of these purchases, or "probes" a crucial factor in establishing the overall position. If at any time the stock goes against you, then wait or close out all your positions, never sustaining more than a 10% loss of invested capital.

* Sell the losers let the winners ride, provided all the factors are positive.

## SUMMARY OF FIVE KEY MONEY MANANGEMENT RULES
*Protect your capital—use probing system to buy
*Observe the 10% bucket shop rule
*Keep cash in reserve

*Stick with the winners—Let your profits ride—Cut your losses

*Take fifty percent of your big winnings off the table

## EMOTIONAL CONTROL

*Emotional control is the most essential factor in playing the market.

*Don't anticipate! Wait until the market gives you the clues, the signals, the hints, before you move. Move only after you have confirmation. Anticipation is the killer. It is the brother to greed and hope. Don't make decisions based on anticipation. The market always gives you time. If you wait for the clues there will be plenty of time to execute your moves.

*All stocks are like human beings, with different personalities: aggressive, reserved, hyper high-strung, direct, dull, old fashioned, futuristic, logical, and illogical. Study the stocks like you would study people, after a while their reactions to certain circumstance become predicable. Some traders limit their trading to stocks in specific price ranges.

* Do not spend a lot of time trying to figure out why the price of a particular stock moves. Rather, examine the facts themselves. The answer lies in *"WHAT"* the tape says not trying to figure out *"WHY,"* and most importantly— *NEVER ARGUE WITH THE TAPE.*

* A stock trader can be convinced to move away from his own convictions by listening to the advice of other traders, persuaded that his judgment may be faulty. Or in the least case, listening to others may cause indecision and bad judgment. This indecision may also cause a loss of confidence, which may well mean a loss of money.

* Tips come from many sources—from a relative, a loved one,

a pal who had just made a serious investment himself and want to pass on his expected good fortune. They also come from hucksters and criminals. Remember:

## ALL TIPS ARE DANGEROUS–TAKE NO TIPS!

* Remove hope from your trading lexicon. Hoping a stock will do something is the true form of gambling. If you do not have good solid reasons for you to hold stock positions then move on to another more logical trade. Wishing a stock up, or down, has caused the downfall of many stock market speculators. Hope walks along hand-in-hand with greed.

*Always be aware of your emotions-don't get too confident over your wins or too despondent over your losses. You must achieve "poise," a balance in your actions.

*NOTHING EVER CHANGES IN THE MARKET— The only thing that changes are the players, and the new players have no financial memory of the previous major cycles, like the crash of 1907, or the crash of 1929, because they have not experienced them. It may be new to the speculator–but it's not new to the market.

* Always have a method of speculating, a plan of attack. And always stick to your plan. Do not constantly change your plan. Find a method that works emotionally and intellectually for you and stick to that method—stick to your own customized rules.

*The speculator is "NOT AN INVESTOR" His object is not to secure a steady return on his money over a long period of time. The speculator must profit by either a rise or fall in the price of whatever he has decided to speculate in.

*Play a lone hand. Make your decisions about your own money

by yourself. Be secretive and silent in your stock trading. Do not disclose your winners or your losers.

*The successful investor is not invested in the market all the time-there are many times when you should be completely in cash. If you are unsure of the direction of the market, wait.

*Never lose control of your emotions when the market moves against you. And never become elated with your successes to such a degree that you think the market is an easy way to make money. Never fight the tape-the tape is the truth...seek harmony with the tape.

*It takes four strong *"mental characteristics"* to be a superior market trader:

*Observation—the ability to observe the facts without prejudice-

*Memory—the ability to remember key events correctly, objectively—

*Mathematics—an easy facility with numbers, at home with digits—

*Experience—to retain and learn from your experiences—

* Livermore believed that subliminal messages, apparent impulses, were nothing more than the subconscious mind talking to him; calling up his experiences, his years of trading. On occasion, Livermore would let his inner-mind lead him, even if he didn't know exactly "why" at the time. Livermore believed Aristotle, who said:

**"WE ARE THE SUM TOTAL OF OUR EXPERIENCE."**

* Emotions must be understood and harnessed before successful speculation is possible:

GREED—is a human emotion existing in all people defined by Webster's dictionary as:

*"The excessive desire for acquiring or possessing, a desire for more than one needs or deserves."* We do not know the origin or blueprint of greed, all we know is that it exists in every person.

FEAR—lays ready to appear in a single heartbeat, and when it does it twists and distorts reason. Reasonable people act unreasonably when they are afraid. And they get afraid every time they start to lose money. Their judgment becomes impaired.

HOPE—Hope lives hand in hand with greed when it comes to the stock market. Once a trade is made hope springs alive. It is man's nature to be hopeful, to be positive, to hope for the best. Hope is essential to the survival of the human race. But hope, like it's stock market cousins, ignorance, greed and fear, distorts reason. Hope clouds facts, and the stock market only deals in facts. Like the spinning of a roulette wheel, the little black ball tells the outcome, not greed, fear, or hope. The result is objective and final with no appeal...like nature.

*Beware of IGNORANCE—The market must be studied and learned, not in a casual way, but in a deep knowledgeable way. The stock market, with its allure of easy money and fast action, induces people into the foolish mis-handling of their money like no other entity. The reverse of ignorance is knowledge, and knowledge is power.

*The stock market is never obvious. It is designed to fool most of the people, most of the time. Livermore's rules are often based on thinking against the grain.

*You should not be in the market all the time. There are times you should be out of the market, for emotional as well as economic reasons.

*When the tape doesn't agree with your decision to buy or sell, wait until it does. Never try to rationalize your position against what the tape is saying.

*Do not give or receive stock tips, just remember: "In a bull market stocks go up-in a bear market they go down. That is all anyone needs to know, or for you to tell them.

*A stock speculator sometimes makes mistakes, and knows that he is making them, but proceeds anyway, only to berate himself later for breaking his own rules—do not break your rules.

*Never become an *"involuntary investor"* by holding a declining stock.

*Never buy a stock on reactions, and never short a stock on rallies.

*Do not use the words "Bullish" or "Bearish." These words fix a firm market-direction in the mind for an extended period of time. Instead use "Upward Trend" and "Downward Trend" when asked the direction you think the market is headed. Simply say: "The line of least resistance is either upward, or downward at this time," as I did.

*Speculation is a business, and like any other business it takes hard work and diligence to succeed.

## Conclusion

"There is nothing new on Wall Street or in stock speculation. What has happened in the past will happen again, and again, and again. This is because human nature does not change, and it is human emotion, solidly built into human nature, that always gets in the way of human intelligence.

**"Of this I am sure."**

**—Jesse Livermore**

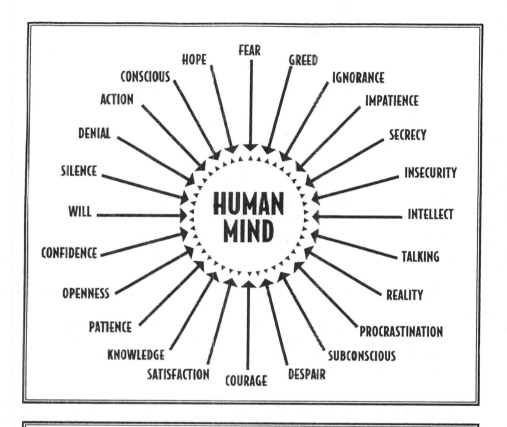

If we visualize the speculator at the center of the wheel, at the hub, we can see the emotional and psychological pressures that must be endured.

For Sigmund Freud, the human psyche is forever and inescapably in conflict by nature - a war that never ends.

For Carl Jung, the successful person ultimately seeks and achieves knowledge, enlightenment and harmony.

Each speculator must determine how they want to deal with their emotions and the psychological slings and arrows of the stock market.

# Software Available Now!—
# Now *You* Can Trade Exactly Like
# The Great Trader "Jesse Livermore"

Richard Smitten, with the help of Dennis Kranyak (U.S. Navy Cmdr.-retired) and well-known trading software code writer Mike Lamont, has developed a complete package of Livermore software exactly as outlined in this book, including:

## Strategy

- For the first time anywhere—Top Down Trading
- Exclusive Livermore Group and Sector Analysis Charts
- Leading Livermore Stock and Sister Stock action
- Special Livermore Scans that put you right in the action when the pivot points first occur

## Money Management and Emotional Control Software

Specially designed software to handle your trades, while incorporating the five rules of money management to ensure you of emotional control by following the rules. Alerts are given to the trader if any of these rules are broken . . . making it easy to stick to the rules.

## Livermore Secrets Revealed

The system includes Livermore's secret mathematical algorithms and the mathematical formulas used by Livermore in his actual trading. These codes are available nowhere else.

Trade like the master, Jesse Livermore, using today's technology.

## Cost

The cost: Only $49.99 per month. To try it, go to the Livermore Web site:

### jesselivermore.com

Join now and put the Livermore trading system to work for you, every day.

# Want to Trade Exactly Like
# Jesse Livermore?

You can with the new software created by Richard Smitten and a number of computer software experts who took five years in the process of developing and duplicating the methods and techniques of Jesse Livermore, including the use of his secret mathematical algorithms. The system is expected to be completed by March 2006.

The system includes all of Livermore's timing systems as well as his money management rules, which assist in a trader's emotional control—as long as you follow the Livermore rules. No more sleepless nights worrying about your trades.

If you are interested in the system, go to the jesselivermore.com Web site or call 772-334-7129

**Remember—Jesse Livermore** is the stock market legend who, with his timing techniques, money management systems, and high-momentum approach to trading in stocks and commodities, was a revolutionary trader whose system remains just as valid in today's trading because:

"The markets change—but human nature never changes."

Jesse Livermore is considered by many of today's top Wall Street traders as the greatest trader who ever lived. For the first time his trading secrets, techniques and stock market methods are revealed. Livermore broke new ground in trading the market. His timing techniques, money management systems, and high-momentum approach to trading in stocks and commodities was revolutionary, and remains valid today.

Livermore ran away from home in 1891 at 14 years of age, with five dollars in his pocket, and immediately started as a board boy in the offices of Paine Weber. He made so much money he was banned from the "Bucket Shops" of Boston and New York. He made a fortune in the crash of 1907, and later lost it, only to make it and lose it several more times.

In the panic of 1907, J.P. Morgan personally implored Livermore to stop selling-short, stop pounding the market into oblivion. He made 3 million dollars in one day during the panic.

He married a beautiful Ziegfield Follies showgirl. They lived in a magnificent mansion on Long Island with 14 servants and a three hundred foot yacht anchored off the back yard that ferried him to Wall Street every morning.

He sold the market short before the crash of 1929, and entered the depression with 100 million in cash.

A mysterious and secret trader he worked out of a palatial penthouse, a highly secure office-fortress on Fifth Avenue. Where he traded in absolute secrecy. Once the market was open no one in the office was allowed to speak until the market closed.

In 1935, Dorothy, his beautiful wife, shot their son, Jesse Livermore Jr., in a heated, drunken argument in Santa Barbara. It was one of the great scandals of the era.

Jesse Livermore ended his own life with a self-inflicted bullet to the brain, ending one of the most dynamic careers in Wall Street history. A complex genius who's life ambition was to win on Wall Street, and he did.

Get the full and personal story of one of the greatest stock market traders who ever lived.

# The Amazing Life of Jesse Livermore: Worlds Greatest Stock Trader

## Quotes—Current Reviews

*"As one of the most shrewd traders of all time, Jesse Livermore demonstrated how important discipline is when trading the market. Richard Smitten's book, "The Amazing Life of Jesse Livermore: World's Greatest Stock Trader," covers how Livermore created his rules.*

*Successful trading is about finding the rules that work and then sticking to those rules. Smitten's book not only covers the strategies that Livermore used in trading the stock market, but also reveals the lessons he learned along the way to develop those strategies."*

—William J. O'neil, Publisher Investor's Business Daily

---

*"After reading Richard Smitten's magnificent biography, two Japanese proverbs came to mind, "Fortune favors the bold" and "Darkness Lies One Inch Ahead." Smitten shows how fortune and darkness were integral parts of Livermore's life.*

*His book has the intrigue of a mystery novel and the lessons of a trading master. What more can one ask for? I eagerly recommend this book to anyone interested in history, the markets and trading psychology."*

—Steve Nison, Author of Japanese Candlestick Charting Techniques

---

*"This is a fascinating account of the rise and fall of the greatest stock trader ever. He knew all of the famous people of his day and saw them all frequently but always remained a man of intriguing mystery. He would not discuss his trades nor the secrets of his success with his friends. "Never give or take market tips," he warns in Richard Smitten's book. When he broke his own rules he paid heavily.*

*"My father E.F. Hutton liked him, backed him and even lent him money twice to get started again after he went broke. Livermore always paid it back and he always regained his trading wealth by going back to his disciplined lone-wolf trading methods. By the time he reached his sixties he had won and lost so monumentally and so often that the thrill of the market's roller coaster ride no longer intrigued him. That was the final blow from which he could not recover. When the excitement of beating the market was gone as was his magic touch and his will to live. That's the sad but poignant lesson in this compelling book.*

—Dina Merrill Hartley

"Great writing. The book is terrific. I started reading it when we took off from Seoul's Kimpo Airport on my way to Germany. By the time we reached Novosibirsk, Russia (five and a half hours later) I had finished it. I just couldn't put it down! Not only is it a great lesson in investing and trading but a fascinating psychological study of what makes a great speculator tick. The rise and fall of a great speculator as well as the rise and fall of his family is great reading. The fact that it is based on interviews with the Livermore's survivors and witnesses to the events make it even more interesting."
—Mark Mobius, Managing Director, Templeton Asset Management

---

"Excellent read! Captures the spirit and times of Jesse Livermore, legendary trader. The book tracks two major market crashes, love affairs, the shooting of Jesse Jr. by his mother, and two family suicides...never a dull moment."
—Ace Greenberg, Chairman Bear Stearns

---

"It is a terrific story well told. I picked it up last night and couldn't put it down until I finished it early this a.m. The Life and Times of Jesse Livermore: The World's Greatest Trader, is an emotional roller coaster. To witness this complex man who is so obviously intelligent, logical, disciplined and driven, repeatedly succeed and fail in the market and marriage is an exciting yet inexpensive way to learn some valuable lesson. If you have any interest in Wall Street, investing, the roaring twenties or the rich and famous of that era, you'll love this book. Certainly today's Momentum Investor will find it worthwhile and perhaps even reassuring."
—Richard Egan, Chairman and Founder, EMC Corporation

---

"This book is a stock market classic! Most entertaining and informative book on the market that I have had the privilege to read in the last 20 years. A must-read for students of the stock market—great even for those who have no knowledge of the market. Grabs you from the start, and holds the reader enthralled from cover to cover. Great book—destined to be a best seller!"
—Dan Sullivan, The Chartist, fund manager/investment advisor

---

My best comment in reading this book, is a resounding "YES!" First, Dick Smitten has pulled together an incredible text on the life and times of Jesse Livermore, and shed some light on how such a successful speculator could become so depressed as to end his own life—something I have always wondered about. But more importantly, this is the first book to really explain the psychology of winning in the markets, as seen and lived through Jesse Livermore. In my own trading, and my writing on SignalWatch.COM, I try to live and trade by the many jewels of trading wisdom so eloquently explained by Jesse and observers around him. I'm tempted to start quoting them here, but you'll just have to read the book. It's an absolutely MUST READ for anyone who is serious about conquering the markets and themselves."
—Ed Downs, CEO Nirvana Systems, author of SignalWatch.com

"*This book is the standard against which all other books on the stock market will be measured. A riveting American tragedy with more emotional turns than a chart on the Dow, and plenty of detailed substance for the market technician interested in uncovering the methodology of the World's Greatest Stock Trader.*"
—Dennis Kranyak, member Society of Market Technicians

---

"*Worth its weight in gold! It is amazing how simple Smitten makes it all seem. Through his research, he has been able to sift through Livermore's complex (and up to now secret) trading techniques. He then has been able to decipher them for all of us to easily understand and allow us to try and "trade like Jesse Livermore," if we want to. We also get a "best-seller novel" roller coaster ride as we journey through Livermore's incredible life and times. A great feat of writing—articulating a very complex set of "formulas" and a very complex man—and its fun!*"
—D. Gordon Badger, First Foundation Capital Canada, Founder

# Livermore Secret Market Key

*Printed exactly*
*as 1940 edition*

# Livermore Market Key

The Livermore Market Key section has been placed in this book exactly as it was written in the 1940 version originally Published by Duell, Sloan and Pearce, New York. All explanatory charts have also been added in their original condition. This section of the book contains reprints of his actual worksheets; complete with Livermore's own day-to-day comments on his system as it applied to actual market action in specific stocks.

The prudent stock market student, after reading and studying this section, will observe that some of the numbers used by Livermore as examples are difficult to follow.

We have attempted to understand these various examples, even so far as going to the second edition which was published in 1966 by Investor's Press, Inc. of Palisades Park, New Jersey. Our objective was to see if there were any problems with the actual worksheets that we may not have noticed in the original 1940 published version.

There were no discrepancies—this is exactly as Livermore presented his Market Key Theory.


RICHARD SMITTEN

# THE LIVERMORE MARKET KEY

MANY years of my life had been devoted to speculation before it dawned upon me that nothing new was happening in the stock market, that price movements were simply being repeated, that while there was variation in different stocks the general price pattern was the same.

The urge fell upon me, as I have said, to keep price records that might be a guide to price movements. This I undertook with some zest. Then I began striving to find a point to start from in helping me to anticipate future movements. That was no easy task.

Now I can look back on those initial efforts and understand why they were not immediately fruitful. Having then a purely speculative mind, I was trying to devise a policy for trading in and out of the market all the time, catching the small intermediate moves. This was wrong, and in time I clearly recognized the fact.

I continued keeping my records, confident that they had a genuine value which only awaited my discovery. At length the secret unfolded. The records told me plainly that they would do nothing for me in the way of intermediate movements. But if I would but use my eyes, I would see the formation of patterns that would foretell major movements.

Right then I determined to eliminate all the minor movements.

By continued close study of the many records I had kept the realization struck me that the *time element* was vital in forming a correct opinion as to the approach of the really important movements. With renewed vigor I concentrated on that feature. What I wanted to discover was a method of recognizing what constituted the minor swings. I realized a market in a definite trend still had numerous intermediate oscillations. They had been confusing. They were no longer to be my concern.

I wanted to find out what constituted the beginning of a Natural Reaction or a Natural Rally. So I began checking the distances of price movements. First I based my calculations on one point. That was no good. Then two points, and so on, until finally I arrived at a point that represented what I thought should constitute the beginning of a Natural Reaction or Natural Rally.

To simplify the picture I had printed a special sheet of paper, ruled in distinctive columns, and so arranged as to give me what I term my Map for Anticipating Future Movements. For each stock I use six columns. Prices are recorded in the columns as they occur. Each column has its heading.

First column is headed Secondary Rally.
Second is headed Natural Rally.
Third is headed Upward Trend.
Fourth is headed Downward Trend.
Fifth is headed Natural Reaction.
Sixth is headed Secondary Reaction.

When figures are recorded in the Upward Trend column they are entered in black ink. In the next two columns to the left I insert the figures in pencil. When figures are recorded in the Downward Trend column they are entered in red ink, and in the next two columns to the right, the entries are also made in pencil.

Thus when recording the prices either in the Upward Trend column or in the Downward Trend column I am impressed with the actual trend at the time. Those figures in distinctive ink talk to me. The red ink or the black ink, used persistently, tells a story that is unmistakable.

When the pencil remains in use I realize I am simply noting the natural oscillations. (In the reproduction of my records later on, bear in mind that the prices entered in light blue ink are those for which I use a pencil on my sheets).

I decided a stock selling around $30.00 or higher would have to rally or react from an extreme point to the extent of approximately six points before I could recognize that a Natural Rally or Natural Reaction was in the making. This rally or reaction does not indicate that the trend of the market has changed its course. It simply indicates that the market is experiencing a natural movement. The trend is exactly the same as it was before the rally or reaction occurred.

I would here explain that I do not take the action of a single stock as an indication that the trend has been positively changed for that group. Instead I take the combined action of two stocks in any group before I recognize the trend has definitely changed, hence the Key Price. By combining the prices and movements in these two stocks I arrive at what I call my Key Price. I find that an individual stock sometimes has a movement big enough to put it in my Upward Trend column or my Downward Trend column. But there is danger of being caught in a false movement by depending upon only one stock. The movement of the two stocks combined gives reasonable assurance. Thus, a positive change of the trend must be confirmed by the action of the Key Price.

Let me illustrate this Key Price method. Strictly adhering to the six-point movement to be used as a basis, you will note in my subsequent records that at times I record a price in U.S.Steel if it only has had a move, let us say, of 5⅛ points because you will find a corresponding movement in Bethlehem Steel, say, of 7 points. Taken together the price movements of the two stocks constitute the Key Price. This Key Price, then, totals twelve points or better, the proper distance required.

When a recording point has been reached—that is, a move of six points average by each of the two stocks—I continue to set down in that same column the extreme price made any day, whenever it is higher than the last price recorded in the Upward Trend column or is lower than the last price recorded in the Downward Trend column. This goes on until a reverse movement starts. This later movement in the other direction will, of course, be based on the same six points average, or twelve points for the Key Price.

You will notice that from then on I never deviate from those points. I make no exceptions. Nor do I make excuses, if the results are not exactly as I anticipated. Remember, these prices I set forth in my records are not my prices. These points have been determined by actual prices registered in the day's trading.

It would be presumptuous for me to say I had arrived at the exact point from which my record of prices should start. It would also be misleading and insincere. I can only say that after years of checking and observation I feel I have arrived somewhere near a point that can be used as a basis for keeping records. From these records one can visualize a map useful in determining the approach of important price movements.

Someone has said that success rides upon the hour of decision.

Certainly success with this plan depends upon courage to act and act promptly when your records tell you to do so. There is no place for vacillation. You must train your mind along those lines. If you are going to wait upon someone else for explanations or reasons or reassurances, the time for action will have escaped.

To give an illustration: After the rapid advance all stocks had following the declaration of war in Europe, a Natural Reaction occurred in the whole market. Then all the stocks in the four prominent groups recovered their reaction and all sold at new high prices—with the exception of the stocks in the Steel group. Anyone keeping records according to my method would have had their attention drawn very forcefully to the action of the Steel stocks. Now there must have been a very good reason why the Steel stocks refused to continue their advance along with the other groups. There was a good reason! But at the time I did not know it, and I doubt very much that anyone could have given a valid explanation for it. However, anyone who had been recording prices would have realized by the action of the Steel stocks that the upward movement in the Steel group had ended. It was not until the middle of January 1940, four months later, that the public was given the facts and the action of the Steel stocks was explained. An announcement was made that during that time the English Government had disposed of over 100,000 shares of U.S. Steel, and in addition Canada had sold 20,000 shares. When that announcement was made the price of U.S. Steel was 26 points lower than its high price attained in September 1939 and Bethlehem Steel was 29 points lower, whereas the prices of the other three prominent groups were off only

2½ to 12¾ points from the high prices that were made at the same time the Steels made their highs. This incident proves the folly of trying to find out "a good reason" why you should buy or sell a given stock. If you wait until you have the reason given you, you will have missed the opportunity of having acted at the proper time! The only reason an investor or speculator should ever want to have pointed out to him is the action of the market itself. Whenever the market does not act right or in the way it should—that is reason enough for you to change your opinion and change it immediately. Remember: there is always a reason for a stock acting the way it does. But also remember: the chances are that you will not become acquainted with that reason until some time in the future, when it is too late to act on it profitably.

I repeat that the formula does not provide points whereby you can make additional trades, with assurance, on intermediate fluctuations which occur during a major move. *The intent is to catch the major moves,* to indicate the beginning and the end of movements of *importance.* And for such purpose you will find the formula of singular value if faithfully pursued. It should, perhaps, also be repeated that this formula is designed for active stocks selling above an approximate price of 30. While the same basic principles are of course operative in anticipating the market action of all stocks, certain adjustments in the formula must be made in considering the very low-priced issues.

There is nothing complicated about it. The various phases will be absorbed quickly and with easy understanding by those who are interested.

In the next chapter is given the exact reproduction of my records, with full explanation of the figures which I have entered.

# EXPLANATORY RULES

1      Record prices in Upward Trend Column in black ink.

2      Record prices in Downward Trend column in red ink.

3      Record prices in the other four columns in pencil.

4 (a)      Draw red lines under your last recorded price in the Upward Trend column the first day you start to record figures in the Natural Reaction column. You begin to do this on the first reaction of approximately six points from the last price recorded in the Upward Trend column.

  (b)      Draw red lines under your last recorded price in the Natural Reaction column the first day you start to record figures in the Natural Rally column or in the Upward Trend column. You begin to do this on the first rally of approximately six points from the last price recorded in the Natural Reaction column.

*You now have two Pivotal Points to watch, and depending on how prices are recorded when the market returns to around one of those points, you will then be able to form an opinion as to whether the positive trend is going to be resumed in earnest—or whether the movement has ended.*

(c) Draw black lines under your last recorded price in the Downward Trend column the first day you start to record figures in the Natural Rally column. You begin to do this on the first rally of approximately six points from the last price recorded in the Downward Trend column.

(d) Draw black lines under your last recorded price in the Natural Rally column the first day you start to record figures in the Natural Reaction column or in the Downward Trend column. You begin to do this on the first reaction of approximately six points from the last price recorded in the Natural Rally column.

5 (a) When recording in the Natural Rally column and a price is reached that is three or more points *above* the last price recorded in the Natural Rally column (with black lines underneath), then that price should be entered in black ink in the Upward Trend column.

(b) When recording in the Natural Reaction column and a price is reached that is three or more points *below* the last price recorded in the Natural Reaction column (with red lines underneath), then that price should be entered in red ink in the Downward Trend column.

6 (a)  When a reaction occurs to an extent of approximately six points, after you have been recording prices in the Upward Trend column, you then start to record those prices in the Natural Reaction column, and continue to do so every day thereafter that the stock sells at a price which is lower than the last recorded price in the Natural Reaction column.

(b)  When a reaction occurs to an extent of approximately six points, after you have been recording prices in the Natural Rally column, you then start to record those prices in the Natural Reaction column, and continue to do so every day thereafter that the stock sells at a price which is lower than the last recorded price in the Natural Reaction column. In case a price is made which is lower than the last recorded price in the Downward Trend column, you would then record that price in the Downward Trend column.

(c)  When a rally occurs to an extent of approximately six points, after you have been recording prices in the Downward Trend column, you then start to record those prices in the Natural Rally column, and continue to do so every day thereafter that the stock sells at a price which is higher than the last recorded price in the Natural Rally column.

(d)  When a rally occurs to an extent of approximately six points, after you have been recording prices in the Natural Reaction column, you then start to record those prices in the Natural Rally column, and continue to do so every day thereafter that the stock sells at a price which is higher than the last recorded price in the Natural Rally column. In case a price is made which is higher than the last recorded price in the Upward Trend column, you would then record that price in the Upward Trend column.

(e) When you start to record figures in the Natural Reaction column and a price is reached *that is lower than the last recorded figure in the Downward Trend column*— then that price should be entered in red ink in the Downward Trend column.

(f) The same rule applies when you are recording figures in the Natural Rally column and a price is reached *that is higher than the last price recorded in the Upward Trend column*—then you would cease recording in the Natural Rally column and record that price in black ink in the Upward Trend column.

(g) In case you had been recording in the Natural Reaction column and a rally should occur of approximately six points from the last recorded figure in the Natural Reaction column—but that price did not exceed the last price recorded in the Natural Rally column—that price should be recorded in the *Secondary* Rally column and should continue to be so recorded until a price had been made which exceeded the last figure recorded in the Natural Rally column. When that occurs, you should commence to record prices in the Naturally Rally column once again.

(h) In case you have been recording in the Natural Rally column and a reaction should occur of approximately six points, but the price reached on that reaction was *not lower* than the last recorded figure in your *Natural* Reaction column—that price should be entered in your *Secondary* Reaction column, and you should continue to record prices in that column until a price was made that was *lower* than the last price recorded in the Natural Reaction column. When that occurs, you should commence to record prices in the Natural Reaction column once again.

7 The same rules apply when recording the Key Price—except that you use twelve points as a basis instead of six points used in individual stocks.

8 The last price recorded in the Downward or Upward Trend columns becomes a Pivotal Point as soon as you begin to record prices in the Natural Rally or Natural Reaction columns. After a rally or reaction has ended you start to record again in the reverse column, and the extreme price made in the previous column then becomes another Pivotal Point.

It is after two Pivotal Point have been reached that these records become of great value to you in helping you anticipate correctly the next movement of importance. These Pivotal Points are drawn to your attention by having a double line drawn underneath them in either red ink or black ink. Those lines are drawn for the express purpose of keeping those points before you, and should be watched very carefully whenever prices are made and recorded near or at one of those points. Your decision to act will then depend on how prices are recorded from then on.

9 (a)   When you see black lines drawn below the last recorded red-ink figure in the Downward Trend column—you *may* be given a signal to buy near that point.

   (b)   When black lines are drawn below a price recorded in the Natural Rally column, and if the stock on its next rally reaches a point near that Pivotal Point price, that is the time you are going to find out whether the market is strong enough definitely to change its course into the Upward Trend column.

   (c)   The reverse holds true when you see red lines drawn under the last price recorded in the Upward Trend column, and when red lines are drawn below the last price recorded in the Natural Reaction column.

10 (a)   This whole method is designed to enable one to see clearly whether a stock is acting the way it ought to, after its first Natural Rally or Reaction has occurred. If the movement is going to be resumed in a positive manner—either up or down—it will carry through its previous Pivotal Point—in individual stocks by three points, or, in the Key Price by six points.

   (b)   If the stock fails to do this—and in a reaction sells three points or more *below* the last Pivotal Point (recorded in the Upward Trend column with red lines drawn underneath), it would indicate that the Upward Trend in the stock is over.

(c) Applying the rule to the Downward Trend: Whenever, after a Natural Rally has ended, new prices are being recorded in the Downward Trend column, these new prices must extend three or more points *below* the last Pivotal Point (with black lines underneath), if the Downward Trend is to be positively resumed.

(d) If the stock fails to do this, and on a rally sells three or more points *above* the last Pivotal Point (recorded in the Downward Trend column with black lines drawn underneath), it would indicate that the Downward Trend in the stock is over.

(e) When recording in the Natural Rally column, if the rally ends a short distance below the last Pivotal Point in the Upward Trend column (with red lines underneath), and the stock reacts three or more points from that price, it is a danger signal, which would indicate the Upward Trend in that stock is over.

(f) When recording in the Natural Reaction column, if the reaction ends a short distance above the last Pivotal Point in the Downward Trend column (with black lines underneath), and the stock rallies three or more points from that price, it is a danger signal, which would indicate the Downward Trend in that stock is over.

# CHARTS AND EXPLANATIONS
FOR THE
## LIVERMORE MARKET KEY

On April 2nd prices began to be recorded in Natural Rally column. Refer to Explanatory Rule 6-B. Draw black line under last price in Downward Trend column. Refer to Explanatory Rule 4-C.

On April 28th, prices began to be recorded in Natural Reaction column. Refer to Explanatory Rule 4-D.

# CHART ONE

| | SECONDARY RALLY | NATURAL RALLY | UPWARD TREND | DOWNWARD TREND | NATURAL REACTION | SECONDARY REACTION | SECONDARY RALLY | NATURAL RALLY | UPWARD TREND | DOWNWARD TREND | NATURAL REACTION | SECONDARY REACTION | SECONDARY RALLY | NATURAL RALLY | UPWARD TREND | DOWNWARD TREND | NATURAL REACTION | SECONDARY REACTION |
|---|---|---|---|---|---|---|---|---|---|---|---|---|---|---|---|---|---|---|
| | | 65 3/4 | | | | | | | | | | | | | | | | |
| | | | | | | | | | 57 | | | | | | 122 3/4 | | | |
| | | | | 48 1/2 | | | | | | | 43 1/4 | | | | | 91 3/4 | | |
| | | 62 1/8 | | | | | | | | | | | | | | | | |
| | | | | | | | | | 65 7/8 | | | | | | 128 | | | |
| | | | | 48 1/4 | | | | | | | 50 1/8 | | | | | | 98 3/8 | |
| 1938 | | | | | | | | 56 7/8 | | | | | | | | | | |
| DATE | | | U.S. STEEL | | | | | | BETHLEHEM STEEL | | | | | | KEY PRICE | | | |
| MAR 23 | | | | 47 | | | | | | | | 50 1/4 | | | | | 97 1/4 | |
| 24 | | | | | | | | | | | | | | | | | | |
| 25 | | | | 44 3/4 | | | | | | 46 3/4 | | | | | | 91 1/2 | | |
| SAT 26 | | | | 44 | | | | | | 46 | | | | | | 90 | | |
| 28 | | | | 43 5/8 | | | | | | | | | | | | 89 5/8 | | |
| 29 | | | | 39 5/8 | | | | | | 43 | | | | | | 82 5/8 | | |
| 30 | | | | 39 | | | | | | 42 1/8 | | | | | | 81 1/8 | | |
| 31 | | | | 38 | | | | | | 40 | | | | | | 78 | | |
| APR 1 | | | | | | | | | | | | | | | | | | |
| SAT 2 | | 43 1/2 | | | | | | 46 3/8 | | | | | | 89 7/8 | | | | |
| 4 | | | | | | | | | | | | | | | | | | |
| 5 | | | | | | | | | | | | | | | | | | |
| 6 | | | | | | | | | | | | | | | | | | |
| 7 | | | | | | | | | | | | | | | | | | |
| 8 | | | | | | | | | | | | | | | | | | |
| SAT 9 | | 46 1/2 | | | | | | 49 3/4 | | | | | | 96 1/4 | | | | |
| 11 | | | | | | | | | | | | | | | | | | |
| 12 | | | | | | | | | | | | | | | | | | |
| 13 | | 47 1/4 | | | | | | | | | | | | 97 | | | | |
| 14 | | 47 1/2 | | | | | | | | | | | | 97 1/4 | | | | |
| SAT 16 | | 49 | | | | | | 52 | | | | | | 101 | | | | |
| 18 | | | | | | | | | | | | | | | | | | |
| 19 | | | | | | | | | | | | | | | | | | |
| 20 | | | | | | | | | | | | | | | | | | |
| 21 | | | | | | | | | | | | | | | | | | |
| 22 | | | | | | | | | | | | | | | | | | |
| SAT 23 | | | | | | | | | | | | | | | | | | |
| 25 | | | | | | | | | | | | | | | | | | |
| 26 | | | | | | | | | | | | | | | | | | |
| 27 | | | | | | | | | | | | | | | | | | |
| 28 | | | | | 43 | | | | | | | | | | | | | |
| 29 | | | | | 42 3/8 | | | | | | 45 | | | | | | 87 3/8 | |
| SAT 30 | | | | | | | | | | | | | | | | | | |
| MAY 2 | | | | | 41 1/2 | | | | | | 44 1/4 | | | | | | 85 3/4 | |
| 3 | | | | | | | | | | | | | | | | | | |
| 4 | | | | | | | | | | | | | | | | | | |

All of these prices recorded are brought forth from the preceding page in order to keep the Pivotal Points always before you.

During the period from May 5th to May 21st inclusive, no prices were recorded because no prices were made lower than the last price recorded in the Natural Reaction column. Nor was there sufficient rally to be recorded.

On May 27th, the price of Bethlehem Steel was recorded in red because it was a lower price than the previous price recorded in the Downward Trend column. Refer to Explanatory Rule 6-C.

On June 2nd, Bethlehem Steel became a buy at 43. Refer to Explanatory Rule 10-C and D. On the same day U. S. Steel became a buy at 42¼. Refer to Explanatory Rule 10-F.

On June 10th, a price was recorded in the Secondary Rally column of Bethlehem Steel. Refer to Explanatory Rule 6-E.

CHART TWO

| | SECONDARY RALLY | NATURAL RALLY | UPWARD TREND | DOWNWARD TREND | NATURAL REACTION | SECONDARY REACTION | SECONDARY RALLY | NATURAL RALLY | UPWARD TREND | DOWNWARD TREND | NATURAL REACTION | SECONDARY REACTION | SECONDARY RALLY | NATURAL RALLY | UPWARD TREND | DOWNWARD TREND | NATURAL REACTION | SECONDARY REACTION |
|---|---|---|---|---|---|---|---|---|---|---|---|---|---|---|---|---|---|---|
| | | | | | | | | | | | | | | | | | | |
| | | | | | | | | | | | | | | | | | | |
| | | | | 38 | | | | | | 40 | | | | | | 78 | | |
| | | 49 | | | | | | 52 | | | | | | 101 | | | | |
| 1938 | | | | | 41½ | | | | | | 44¼ | | | | | | 85¾ | |
| DATE | | | U.S. STEEL | | | | | | BETHLEHEM STEEL | | | | | | KEY PRICE | | | |
| MAY 5 | | | | | | | | | | | | | | | | | | |
| 6 | | | | | | | | | | | | | | | | | | |
| SAT. 7 | | | | | | | | | | | | | | | | | | |
| 9 | | | | | | | | | | | | | | | | | | |
| 10 | | | | | | | | | | | | | | | | | | |
| 11 | | | | | | | | | | | | | | | | | | |
| 12 | | | | | | | | | | | | | | | | | | |
| 13 | | | | | | | | | | | | | | | | | | |
| SAT. 14 | | | | | | | | | | | | | | | | | | |
| 16 | | | | | | | | | | | | | | | | | | |
| 17 | | | | | | | | | | | | | | | | | | |
| 18 | | | | | | | | | | | | | | | | | | |
| 19 | | | | | | | | | | | | | | | | | | |
| 20 | | | | | | | | | | | | | | | | | | |
| SAT. 21 | | | | | | | | | | | | | | | | | | |
| 23 | | | | | | | | | | | 44⅛ | | | | | | 85⅝ | |
| 24 | | | | | | | | | | | 43½ | | | | | | 85 | |
| 25 | | | | | 41⅜ | | | | | | 42½ | | | | | | 83⅞ | |
| 26 | | | | | 40⅛ | | | | | | 40½ | | | | | | 80⅝ | |
| 27 | | | | | 39⅞ | | | | | 39¾ | | | | | | | 79⅝ | |
| SAT. 28 | | | | | | | | | | | | | | | | | | |
| 31 | | | | | 39¼ | | | | | | | | | | | | 79 | |
| JUNE 1 | | | | | | | | | | | | | | | | | | |
| 2 | | | | | | | | | | | | | | | | | | |
| 3 | | | | | | | | | | | | | | | | | | |
| SAT. 4 | | | | | | | | | | | | | | | | | | |
| 6 | | | | | | | | | | | | | | | | | | |
| 7 | | | | | | | | | | | | | | | | | | |
| 8 | | | | | | | | | | | | | | | | | | |
| 9 | | | | | | | | | | | | | | | | | | |
| 10 | | | | | | | 46½ | | | | | | | | | | | |
| SAT. 11 | | | | | | | | | | | | | | | | | | |
| 13 | | | | | | | | | | | | | | | | | | |
| 14 | | | | | | | | | | | | | | | | | | |
| 15 | | | | | | | | | | | | | | | | | | |
| 16 | | | | | | | | | | | | | | | | | | |

On June 20th, the price of U.S. Steel was recorded in the Secondary Rally column. Refer to Explanatory Rule 6-G.

On June 24th, prices of U.S. Steel and Bethlehem Steel were recorded in black ink in the Upward Trend column. Refer to Explanatory Rule 5-A.

On July 11th, prices of U.S. Steel and Bethlehem Steel were recorded in the Natural Reaction column. Refer to Explanatory Rules 6-A and 4-A.

On July 19th, prices of U.S. Steel and Bethlehem Steel were recorded in the Upward Trend column in black ink because those prices were higher than the last prices that were recorded in those columns. Refer to Explanatory Rule 4-B.

# CHART THREE

| | SECONDARY RALLY | NATURAL RALLY | UPWARD TREND | DOWNWARD TREND | NATURAL REACTION | SECONDARY REACTION | SECONDARY RALLY | NATURAL RALLY | UPWARD TREND | DOWNWARD TREND | NATURAL REACTION | SECONDARY REACTION | SECONDARY RALLY | NATURAL RALLY | UPWARD TREND | DOWNWARD TREND | NATURAL REACTION | SECONDARY REACTION |
|---|---|---|---|---|---|---|---|---|---|---|---|---|---|---|---|---|---|---|
| | | | | 38 | | | | | | 40 | | | | | | 78 | | |
| | | 49 | | | | | | 52 | | | | | | 101 | | | | |
| | | | | $39\frac{1}{4}$ | | | | | | $39\frac{3}{4}$ | | | | | | | 79 | |
| 1938 | | | | | $46\frac{1}{2}$ | | | | | | | | | | | | | |
| DATE | | U.S. STEEL | | | | | | BETHLEHEM STEEL | | | | | | KEY PRICE | | | | |
| JUNE 17 | | | | | | | | | | | | | | | | | | |
| SAT.18 | | | | | | | | | | | | | | | | | | |
| 20 | $45\frac{3}{8}$ | | | | | | $48\frac{1}{4}$ | | | | | | $93\frac{5}{8}$ | | | | | |
| 21 | $46\frac{1}{2}$ | | | | | | $49\frac{7}{8}$ | | | | | | $96\frac{3}{4}$ | | | | | |
| 22 | $48\frac{1}{2}$ | | | | | | $50\frac{7}{8}$ | | | | | | $99\frac{3}{8}$ | | | | | |
| 23 | | $51\frac{1}{4}$ | | | | | | $53\frac{1}{4}$ | | | | | | $104\frac{1}{2}$ | | | | |
| 24 | | | $53\frac{3}{4}$ | | | | | | $55\frac{1}{8}$ | | | | | | $108\frac{7}{8}$ | | | |
| SAT.25 | | | $54\frac{7}{8}$ | | | | | | $58\frac{1}{8}$ | | | | | | 113 | | | |
| 27 | | | | | | | | | | | | | | | | | | |
| 28 | | | | | | | | | | | | | | | | | | |
| 29 | | | $56\frac{7}{8}$ | | | | | | $60\frac{1}{8}$ | | | | | | 117 | | | |
| 30 | | | $58\frac{3}{8}$ | | | | | | $61\frac{5}{8}$ | | | | | | 120 | | | |
| JULY 1 | | | 59 | | | | | | | | | | | | $120\frac{5}{8}$ | | | |
| SAT.2 | | | $60\frac{7}{8}$ | | | | | | $62\frac{1}{2}$ | | | | | | $123\frac{3}{8}$ | | | |
| 5 | | | | | | | | | | | | | | | | | | |
| 6 | | | | | | | | | | | | | | | | | | |
| 7 | | | $61\frac{3}{4}$ | | | | | | | | | | | | $124\frac{1}{4}$ | | | |
| 8 | | | | | | | | | | | | | | | | | | |
| SAT.9 | | | | | | | | | | | | | | | | | | |
| 11 | | | | $55\frac{5}{8}$ | | | | | | $56\frac{3}{4}$ | | | | | | $112\frac{7}{8}$ | | |
| 12 | | | | $55\frac{1}{2}$ | | | | | | | | | | | | $112\frac{1}{4}$ | | |
| 13 | | | | | | | | | | | | | | | | | | |
| 14 | | | | | | | | | | | | | | | | | | |
| 15 | | | | | | | | | | | | | | | | | | |
| SAT.16 | | | | | | | | | | | | | | | | | | |
| 18 | | | | | | | | | | | | | | | | | | |
| 19 | | | $62\frac{3}{4}$ | | | | | | $63\frac{3}{8}$ | | | | | | $125\frac{1}{2}$ | | | |
| 20 | | | | | | | | | | | | | | | | | | |
| 21 | | | | | | | | | | | | | | | | | | |
| 22 | | | | | | | | | | | | | | | | | | |
| SAT.23 | | | | | | | | | | | | | | | | | | |
| 25 | | | $63\frac{3}{4}$ | | | | | | | | | | | | $126\frac{3}{4}$ | | | |
| 26 | | | | | | | | | | | | | | | | | | |
| 27 | | | | | | | | | | | | | | | | | | |
| 28 | | | | | | | | | | | | | | | | | | |
| 29 | | | | | | | | | | | | | | | | | | |

On August 12th, the price of U. S. Steel was recorded in the Secondary Reaction column because the price was not lower than the last price previously recorded in the Natural Reaction column. On the same day the price of Bethlehem Steel was recorded in the Natural Reaction column because that price was lower than the last price previously recorded in the Natural Reaction column.

On August 24th, prices of U. S. Steel and Bethlehem Steel were recorded in the Natural Rally column. Refer to Explanatory Rule 6-D.

On August 29th, prices of U. S. Steel and Bethlehem Steel were recorded in the Secondary Reaction column. Refer to Explanatory Rule 6-H.

# CHART FOUR

| | SECONDARY RALLY | NATURAL RALLY | UPWARD TREND | DOWNWARD TREND | NATURAL REACTION | SECONDARY REACTION | SECONDARY RALLY | NATURAL RALLY | UPWARD TREND | DOWNWARD TREND | NATURAL REACTION | SECONDARY REACTION | SECONDARY RALLY | NATURAL RALLY | UPWARD TREND | DOWNWARD TREND | NATURAL REACTION | SECONDARY REACTION |
|---|---|---|---|---|---|---|---|---|---|---|---|---|---|---|---|---|---|---|
| | | | 61 3/4 | | | | | | 62 1/2 | | | | | | 124 1/4 | | | |
| | | | | | 55 1/2 | | | | | | 56 3/4 | | | | | | 112 1/4 | |
| | | | 63 1/4 | | | | | | 63 1/8 | | | | | | 126 3/8 | | | |
| | | | | | | | | | | | | | | | | | | |
| 1938 | | | | | | | | | | | | | | | | | | |
| DATE | | | U.S. STEEL | | | | | | BETHLEHEM STEEL | | | | | | KEY PRICE | | | |
| SAT. JULY 30 | | | | | | | | | | | | | | | | | | |
| AUG. 1 | | | | | | | | | | | | | | | | | | |
| 2 | | | | | | | | | | | | | | | | | | |
| 3 | | | | | | | | | | | | | | | | | | |
| 4 | | | | | | | | | | | | | | | | | | |
| 5 | | | | | | | | | | | | | | | | | | |
| SAT. 6 | | | | | | | | | | | | | | | | | | |
| 8 | | | | | | | | | | | | | | | | | | |
| 9 | | | | | | | | | | | | | | | | | | |
| 10 | | | | | | | | | | | | | | | | | | |
| 11 | | | | | | | | | | | | | | | | | | |
| 12 | | | | | | 56 5/8 | | | | | 54 7/8 | | | | | | 111 1/2 | |
| SAT. 13 | | | | | | 56 1/2 | | | | | 54 5/8 | | | | | | 111 1/8 | |
| 15 | | | | | | | | | | | | | | | | | | |
| 16 | | | | | | | | | | | | | | | | | | |
| 17 | | | | | | | | | | | | | | | | | | |
| 18 | | | | | | | | | | | | | | | | | | |
| 19 | | | | | | | | | | | | | | | | | | |
| SAT. 20 | | | | | | | | | | | | | | | | | | |
| 22 | | | | | | | | | | | | | | | | | | |
| 23 | | | | | | | | | | | | | | | | | | |
| 24 | | 61 5/8 | | | | | | 61 3/8 | | | | | | 123 | | | | |
| 25 | | | | | | | | | | | | | | | | | | |
| 26 | | 61 7/8 | | | | | | 61 1/2 | | | | | | 123 3/8 | | | | |
| SAT. 27 | | | | | | | | | | | | | | | | | | |
| 29 | | | | | | 56 1/8 | | | | | | 55 | | | | | — | |
| 30 | | | | | | | | | | | | | | | | | | |
| 31 | | | | | | | | | | | | | | | | | | |
| SEPT. 1 | | | | | | | | | | | | | | | | | | |
| 2 | | | | | | | | | | | | | | | | | | |
| SAT. 3 | | | | | | | | | | | | | | | | | | |
| 6 | | | | | | | | | | | | | | | | | | |
| 7 | | | | | | | | | | | | | | | | | | |
| 8 | | | | | | | | | | | | | | | | | | |
| 9 | | | | | | | | | | | | | | | | | | |
| SAT. 10 | | | | | | | | | | | | | | | | | | |

On September 14th, the price of U. S. Steel was recorded in the Downward Trend column. Refer to Explanatory Rule 5-B. On the same day a price was recorded in the Natural Reaction column of Bethlehem Steel. That price was still being recorded in the Natural Reaction column because it had not reached a price that was 3 points lower than its previous price with red lines drawn. On September 20th, prices of U. S. Steel and Bethlehem Steel were recorded in the Natural Rally column. Refer to Explanatory Rule 6-C for U. S. Steel and 6-D for Bethlehem Steel.

On September 24th, the price of U. S. Steel was recorded in the Downward Trend column in red ink, being a new price in that column.

On September 29th, prices of U. S. Steel and Bethlehem Steel were recorded in the Secondary Rally column. Refer to Explanatory Rule 6-G.

On October 5th, the price of U. S. Steel was recorded in the Upward Trend column in black ink. Refer to Explanatory Rule 5-A.

On October 8th, the price of Bethlehem Steel was recorded in the Upward Trend column in black ink. Refer to Explanatory Rule 6-D.

# CHART FIVE

| | SECONDARY RALLY | NATURAL RALLY | UPWARD TREND | DOWNWARD TREND | NATURAL REACTION | SECONDARY REACTION | SECONDARY RALLY | NATURAL RALLY | UPWARD TREND | DOWNWARD TREND | NATURAL REACTION | SECONDARY REACTION | SECONDARY RALLY | NATURAL RALLY | UPWARD TREND | DOWNWARD TREND | NATURAL REACTION | SECONDARY REACTION |
|---|---|---|---|---|---|---|---|---|---|---|---|---|---|---|---|---|---|---|
| | | | 63¼ | | | | | | 63⅛ | | | | | | 126⅝ | | | |
| | | | | | 55½ | | | | | | 54⅜ | | | | | | 111⅛ | |
| | | | | | | | | 61½ | | | | | | 123⅜ | | | | |
| | | 61⅞ | | | | | | | | | | | | | | | | |
| 1938 | | | | | | 56⅛ | | | | | | 55 | | | | | | |
| DATE | | | U.S. STEEL | | | | | | BETHLEHEM STEEL | | | | | | KEY PRICE | | | |
| SEPT. 12 | | | | | | | | | | | | | | | | | | |
| 13 | | | | | 54¼ | | | | | | 53⅝ | | | | | | 107⅞ | |
| 14 | | | | 52 | | | | | | | 52½ | | | | | 104½ | | |
| 15 | | | | | | | | | | | | | | | | | | |
| 16 | | | | | | | | | | | | | | | | | | |
| SAT. 17 | | | | | | | | | | | | | | | | | | |
| 19 | | | | | | | | | | | | | | | | | | |
| 20 | | 57⅝ | | | | | | 58¼ | | | | | | | | | | |
| 21 | | 58 | | | | | | | | | | | | 116¼ | | | | |
| 22 | | | | | | | | | | | | | | | | | | |
| 23 | | | | | | | | | | | | | | | | | | |
| SAT. 24 | | | | 51⅞ | | | | | | | 52 | | | | | 103⅞ | | |
| 26 | | | | 51⅛ | | | | | | | 51¼ | | | | | 102⅜ | | |
| 27 | | | | | | | | | | | | | | | | | | |
| 28 | | | | 50⅞ | | | | | | | 51 | | | | | 101⅞ | | |
| 29 | 57⅛ | | | | | | 57¾ | | | | | | 114⅞ | | | | | |
| 30 | | 59¼ | | | | | | 59½ | | | | | | 118¾ | | | | |
| SAT. OCT. 1 | | 60¼ | | | | | | 60 | | | | | | 120¼ | | | | |
| 3 | | 60⅜ | | | | | | 60⅜ | | | | | | 120¾ | | | | |
| 4 | | | | | | | | | | | | | | | | | | |
| 5 | | | 62 | | | | | 62 | | | | | | | 124 | | | |
| 6 | | | 63 | | | | | 63 | | | | | | | 126 | | | |
| 7 | | | | | | | | | | | | | | | | | | |
| SAT. 8 | | | 64¼ | | | | | | 64 | | | | | | 128¼ | | | |
| 10 | | | | | | | | | | | | | | | | | | |
| 11 | | | | | | | | | | | | | | | | | | |
| 13 | | | 65⅜ | | | | | | 65⅛ | | | | | | 130½ | | | |
| 14 | | | | | | | | | | | | | | | | | | |
| SAT. 15 | | | | | | | | | | | | | | | | | | |
| 17 | | | | | | | | | | | | | | | | | | |
| 18 | | | | | | | | | | | | | | | | | | |
| 19 | | | | | | | | | | | | | | | | | | |
| 20 | | | | | | | | | | | | | | | | | | |
| 21 | | | | | | | | | | | | | | | | | | |
| SAT. 22 | | | 65⅞ | | | | | | 67½ | | | | | | 133⅜ | | | |
| 24 | | | 66 | | | | | | | | | | | | 133½ | | | |

On November 18th, prices of U. S. Steel and Bethlehem Steel were recorded in the Natural Reaction column. Refer to Explanatory Rule 6-A.

## CHART SIX

| DATE | SECONDARY RALLY | NATURAL RALLY | UPWARD TREND | DOWNWARD TREND | NATURAL REACTION | SECONDARY REACTION | SECONDARY RALLY | NATURAL RALLY | UPWARD TREND | DOWNWARD TREND | NATURAL REACTION | SECONDARY REACTION | SECONDARY RALLY | NATURAL RALLY | UPWARD TREND | DOWNWARD TREND | NATURAL REACTION | SECONDARY REACTION |
|---|---|---|---|---|---|---|---|---|---|---|---|---|---|---|---|---|---|---|
| 1938 | | | $66$ | | | | | | $67\frac{1}{2}$ | | | | | | $133\frac{1}{2}$ | | | |
| DATE | | | U.S. STEEL | | | | | | BETHLEHEM STEEL | | | | | | KEY PRICE | | | |
| OCT.25 | | | $66\frac{1}{8}$ | | | | | | $67\frac{3}{4}$ | | | | | | $134$ | | | |
| 26 | | | | | | | | | | | | | | | | | | |
| 27 | | | $66\frac{1}{2}$ | | | | | | $68\frac{7}{8}$ | | | | | | $135\frac{3}{4}$ | | | |
| 28 | | | | | | | | | | | | | | | | | | |
| SAT.29 | | | | | | | | | | | | | | | | | | |
| 31 | | | | | | | | | | | | | | | | | | |
| NOV.1 | | | | | | | | | $69$ | | | | | | $135\frac{1}{2}$ | | | |
| 2 | | | | | | | | | | | | | | | | | | |
| 3 | | | | | | | | | $69\frac{1}{2}$ | | | | | | $136$ | | | |
| 4 | | | | | | | | | | | | | | | | | | |
| SAT.5 | | | | | | | | | | | | | | | | | | |
| 7 | | | $66\frac{3}{4}$ | | | | | | $71\frac{7}{8}$ | | | | | | $138\frac{5}{8}$ | | | |
| 9 | | | $69\frac{1}{2}$ | | | | | | $75\frac{3}{8}$ | | | | | | $144\frac{7}{8}$ | | | |
| 10 | | | $70$ | | | | | | $75\frac{1}{2}$ | | | | | | $145\frac{1}{2}$ | | | |
| SAT.12 | | | $71\frac{1}{4}$ | | | | | | $77\frac{5}{8}$ | | | | | | $148\frac{7}{8}$ | | | |
| 14 | | | | | | | | | | | | | | | | | | |
| 15 | | | | | | | | | | | | | | | | | | |
| 16 | | | | | | | | | | | | | | | | | | |
| 17 | | | | | | | | | | | | | | | | | | |
| 18 | | | | $65\frac{1}{8}$ | | | | | | $71\frac{7}{8}$ | | | | | | | $137$ | |
| SAT.19 | | | | | | | | | | | | | | | | | | |
| 21 | | | | | | | | | | | | | | | | | | |
| 22 | | | | | | | | | | | | | | | | | | |
| 23 | | | | | | | | | | | | | | | | | | |
| 25 | | | | | | | | | | | | | | | | | | |
| SAT.26 | | | | $63\frac{1}{4}$ | | | | | | $71\frac{1}{2}$ | | | | | | | $134\frac{3}{4}$ | |
| 28 | | | | $61$ | | | | | | $68\frac{3}{4}$ | | | | | | | $129\frac{3}{4}$ | |
| 29 | | | | | | | | | | | | | | | | | | |
| 30 | | | | | | | | | | | | | | | | | | |
| DEC.1 | | | | | | | | | | | | | | | | | | |
| 2 | | | | | | | | | | | | | | | | | | |
| SAT.3 | | | | | | | | | | | | | | | | | | |
| 5 | | | | | | | | | | | | | | | | | | |
| 6 | | | | | | | | | | | | | | | | | | |
| 7 | | | | | | | | | | | | | | | | | | |
| 8 | | | | | | | | | | | | | | | | | | |

On December 14th, prices of U. S. Steel and Bethlehem Steel were recorded in the Natural Rally column. Refer to Explanatory Rule 6-D.

On December 28th, the price of Bethlehem Steel was recorded in the Upward Trend column in black ink, being a price higher than the last price previously recorded in that column.

On January 4th, the next trend of the market was being indicated according to the Livermore method. Refer to Explanatory Rules 10-A and B.

On January 12th, prices of U. S. Steel and Bethlehem Steel were recorded in the Secondary Reaction column. Refer to Explanatory Rule 6-H.

## CHART SEVEN

| Date | Secondary Rally | Natural Rally | Upward Trend | Downward Trend | Natural Reaction | Secondary Reaction | Secondary Rally | Natural Rally | Upward Trend | Downward Trend | Natural Reaction | Secondary Reaction | Secondary Rally | Natural Rally | Upward Trend | Downward Trend | Natural Reaction | Secondary Reaction |
|---|---|---|---|---|---|---|---|---|---|---|---|---|---|---|---|---|---|---|
| | | | $71\frac{1}{4}$ | | | | | | $77\frac{5}{8}$ | | | | | | $148\frac{7}{8}$ | | | |
| | | | | 61 | | | | | | | $68\frac{3}{4}$ | | | | | | $129\frac{3}{4}$ | |
| 1938 DATE | | | U.S. STEEL | | | | | | BETHLEHEM STEEL | | | | | | KEY PRICE | | | |
| DEC 9 | | | | | | | | | | | | | | | | | | |
| SAT 10 | | | | | | | | | | | | | | | | | | |
| 12 | | | | | | | | | | | | | | | | | | |
| 13 | | | | | | | | | | | | | | | | | | |
| 14 | | $66\frac{5}{8}$ | | | | | | $75\frac{1}{4}$ | | | | | | $141\frac{7}{8}$ | | | | |
| 15 | | $67\frac{7}{8}$ | | | | | | $76\frac{3}{8}$ | | | | | | $143\frac{1}{2}$ | | | | |
| 16 | | | | | | | | | | | | | | | | | | |
| SAT 17 | | | | | | | | | | | | | | | | | | |
| 19 | | | | | | | | | | | | | | | | | | |
| 20 | | | | | | | | | | | | | | | | | | |
| 21 | | | | | | | | | | | | | | | | | | |
| 22 | | | | | | | | | | | | | | | | | | |
| 23 | | | | | | | | | | | | | | | | | | |
| SAT 24 | | | | | | | | | | | | | | | | | | |
| 27 | | | | | | | | | | | | | | | | | | |
| 28 | | $67\frac{3}{4}$ | | | | | | 78 | | | | | | $145\frac{3}{4}$ | | | | |
| 29 | | | | | | | | | | | | | | | | | | |
| 30 | | | | | | | | | | | | | | | | | | |
| SAT 31 | | | | | | | | | | | | | | | | | | |
| 1939 JAN 3 | | | | | | | | | | | | | | | | | | |
| 4 | | 70 | | | | | | 80 | | | | | | 150 | | | | |
| 5 | | | | | | | | | | | | | | | | | | |
| 6 | | | | | | | | | | | | | | | | | | |
| SAT 7 | | | | | | | | | | | | | | | | | | |
| 9 | | | | | | | | | | | | | | | | | | |
| 10 | | | | | | | | | | | | | | | | | | |
| 11 | | | | | | | | | | | | $73\frac{3}{4}$ | | | | | | |
| 12 | | | | | | $62\frac{5}{8}$ | | | | | $71\frac{1}{2}$ | | | | | | | $139\frac{1}{8}$ |
| 13 | | | | | | | | | | | | | | | | | | |
| SAT 14 | | | | | | | | | | | | | | | | | | |
| 16 | | | | | | | | | | | | | | | | | | |
| 17 | | | | | | | | | | | | | | | | | | |
| 18 | | | | | | | | | | | | | | | | | | |
| 19 | | | | | | | | | | | | | | | | | | |
| 20 | | | | | | | | | | | | | | | | | | |
| SAT 21 | | | | | 62 | | | | | | $69\frac{1}{2}$ | | | | | | | $131\frac{1}{2}$ |

On January 23rd, prices of U. S. Steel and Bethlehem Steel were recorded in the Downward Trend column. Refer to Explanatory Rule 5-B.


On January 31st, prices of U. S. Steel and Bethlehem Steel were recorded in the Natural Rally column. Refer to Explanatory Rules 6-C and 4-C.

# CHART EIGHT

| DATE | SECONDARY RALLY | NATURAL RALLY | UPWARD TREND | DOWNWARD TREND | NATURAL REACTION | SECONDARY REACTION | SECONDARY RALLY | NATURAL RALLY | UPWARD TREND | DOWNWARD TREND | NATURAL REACTION | SECONDARY REACTION | SECONDARY RALLY | NATURAL RALLY | UPWARD TREND | DOWNWARD TREND | NATURAL REACTION | SECONDARY REACTION |
|---|---|---|---|---|---|---|---|---|---|---|---|---|---|---|---|---|---|---|
| | | | $71\frac{1}{4}$ | | | | | | $77\frac{5}{8}$ | | | | | | $148\frac{7}{8}$ | | | |
| | | | | $61$ | | | | | | | $68\frac{3}{4}$ | | | | | | $129\frac{3}{4}$ | |
| | | $70$ | | | | | | $80$ | | | | | | $150$ | | | | |
| 1939 | | | | | $62$ | | | | | | $69\frac{1}{2}$ | | | | | | | $131\frac{1}{2}$ |
| | | | U.S. STEEL | | | | | | BETHLEHEM STEEL | | | | | | KEY PRICE | | | |
| JAN 23 | | | $57\frac{7}{8}$ | | | | | | $63\frac{3}{4}$ | | | | | | $121\frac{5}{8}$ | | | |
| 24 | | | $56\frac{1}{2}$ | | | | | | $63\frac{1}{4}$ | | | | | | $119\frac{3}{4}$ | | | |
| 25 | | | $55\frac{5}{8}$ | | | | | | $63$ | | | | | | $118\frac{5}{8}$ | | | |
| 26 | | | $53\frac{1}{4}$ | | | | | | $60\frac{1}{4}$ | | | | | | $113\frac{1}{2}$ | | | |
| 27 | | | | | | | | | | | | | | | | | | |
| SAT 28 | | | | | | | | | | | | | | | | | | |
| 30 | | | | | | | | | | | | | | | | | | |
| 31 | | $59\frac{1}{2}$ | | | | | | $68\frac{1}{2}$ | | | | | | $128$ | | | | |
| FEB 1 | | | | | | | | | | | | | | | | | | |
| 2 | | $60$ | | | | | | | | | | | | $128\frac{1}{2}$ | | | | |
| 3 | | | | | | | | | | | | | | | | | | |
| SAT 4 | | $60\frac{5}{8}$ | | | | | | $69$ | | | | | | $129\frac{5}{8}$ | | | | |
| 6 | | | | | | | | $69\frac{7}{8}$ | | | | | | $130\frac{3}{4}$ | | | | |
| 7 | | | | | | | | | | | | | | | | | | |
| 8 | | | | | | | | | | | | | | | | | | |
| 9 | | | | | | | | | | | | | | | | | | |
| 10 | | | | | | | | | | | | | | | | | | |
| SAT 11 | | | | | | | | | | | | | | | | | | |
| 14 | | | | | | | | | | | | | | | | | | |
| 15 | | | | | | | | | | | | | | | | | | |
| 16 | | | | | | | | $70\frac{3}{4}$ | | | | | | $131\frac{5}{8}$ | | | | |
| 17 | | $61\frac{1}{8}$ | | | | | | $71\frac{1}{4}$ | | | | | | $132\frac{3}{8}$ | | | | |
| SAT 18 | | $61\frac{1}{4}$ | | | | | | | | | | | | $132\frac{1}{2}$ | | | | |
| 20 | | | | | | | | | | | | | | | | | | |
| 21 | | | | | | | | | | | | | | | | | | |
| 23 | | | | | | | | | | | | | | | | | | |
| 24 | | $62\frac{1}{4}$ | | | | | | $72\frac{3}{8}$ | | | | | | $139\frac{5}{8}$ | | | | |
| SAT 25 | | $63\frac{3}{4}$ | | | | | | $74\frac{1}{4}$ | | | | | | $138\frac{1}{2}$ | | | | |
| 27 | | | | | | | | | | | | | | | | | | |
| 28 | | $64\frac{3}{4}$ | | | | | | $75$ | | | | | | $139\frac{3}{4}$ | | | | |
| MAR 1 | | | | | | | | | | | | | | | | | | |
| 2 | | | | | | | | | | | | | | | | | | |
| 3 | | $64\frac{7}{8}$ | | | | | | $75\frac{1}{4}$ | | | | | | $140$ | | | | |
| SAT 4 | | | | | | | | $75\frac{1}{2}$ | | | | | | $140\frac{3}{8}$ | | | | |
| 6 | | | | | | | | | | | | | | | | | | |
| 7 | | | | | | | | | | | | | | | | | | |

On March 16th, prices of U. S. Steel and Bethlehem Steel were recorded in the Natural Reaction column. Refer to Explanatory Rule 6-B.

On March 30th, the price of U. S. Steel was recorded in the Downward Trend column, being a lower price than was previously recorded in the Downward Trend column.

On March 31st, the price of Bethlehem Steel was recorded in the Downward Trend column, being a lower price than was previously recorded in the Downward Trend column.

On April 15th, prices of U. S. Steel and Bethlehem Steel were recorded in the Natural Rally column. Refer to Explanatory Rule 6-C.

# CHART NINE

| | Secondary Rally | Natural Rally | Upward Trend | Downward Trend | Natural Reaction | Secondary Reaction | Secondary Rally | Natural Rally | Upward Trend | Downward Trend | Natural Reaction | Secondary Reaction | Secondary Rally | Natural Rally | Upward Trend | Downward Trend | Natural Reaction | Secondary Reaction |
|---|---|---|---|---|---|---|---|---|---|---|---|---|---|---|---|---|---|---|
| | | | | 53 1/4 | | | | | | 60 1/4 | | | | | | 113 1/2 | | |
| 1939 | | 64 7/8 | | | | | | 75 1/2 | | | | | | 140 3/8 | | | | |
| DATE | | | U.S. STEEL | | | | | | BETHLEHEM STEEL | | | | | | KEY PRICE | | | |
| MAR. 8 | | 65 | | | | | | | | | | | | 140 1/2 | | | | |
| 9 | | 65 1/2 | | | | | | 75 7/8 | | | | | | 141 3/8 | | | | |
| 10 | | | | | | | | | | | | | | | | | | |
| SAT. 11 | | | | | | | | | | | | | | | | | | |
| 13 | | | | | | | | | | | | | | | | | | |
| 14 | | | | | | | | | | | | | | | | | | |
| 15 | | | | | | | | | | | | | | | | | | |
| 16 | | | | | 59 5/8 | | | | | | 69 1/4 | | | | | | 128 7/8 | |
| 17 | | | | | 56 3/4 | | | | | | 66 3/4 | | | | | | 123 1/2 | |
| SAT. 18 | | | | | 54 3/4 | | | | | | 65 | | | | | | 119 3/4 | |
| 20 | | | | | | | | | | | | | | | | | | |
| 21 | | | | | | | | | | | | | | | | | | |
| 22 | | | | | 53 1/2 | | | | | | 63 5/8 | | | | | | 117 1/8 | |
| 23 | | | | | | | | | | | | | | | | | | |
| 24 | | | | | | | | | | | | | | | | | | |
| SAT. 25 | | | | | | | | | | | | | | | | | | |
| 27 | | | | | | | | | | | | | | | | | | |
| 28 | | | | | | | | | | | | | | | | | | |
| 29 | | | | | | | | | | | | | | | | | | |
| 30 | | | | 52 1/8 | | | | | | | 62 | | | | | | 114 1/8 | |
| 31 | | | | 49 7/8 | | | | | | 58 3/4 | | | | | | 108 5/8 | | |
| APR. SAT. 1 | | | | | | | | | | | | | | | | | | |
| 3 | | | | | | | | | | | | | | | | | | |
| 4 | | | | 48 1/4 | | | | | | 57 5/8 | | | | | | 105 7/8 | | |
| 5 | | | | | | | | | | | | | | | | | | |
| 6 | | | | 47 1/4 | | | | | | 55 1/2 | | | | | | 102 3/4 | | |
| SAT. 8 | | | | 44 7/8 | | | | | | 52 1/2 | | | | | | 97 3/8 | | |
| 10 | | | | | | | | | | | | | | | | | | |
| 11 | | | | 44 3/8 | | | | | | 51 5/8 | | | | | | 96 | | |
| 12 | | | | | | | | | | | | | | | | | | |
| 13 | | | | | | | | | | | | | | | | | | |
| 14 | | | | | | | | | | | | | | | | | | |
| SAT 15 | | 50 | | | | | | 58 1/2 | | | | | | 108 1/2 | | | | |
| 17 | | | | | | | | | | | | | | | | | | |
| 18 | | | | | | | | | | | | | | | | | | |
| 19 | | | | | | | | | | | | | | | | | | |

On May 17th, prices of U. S. Steel and Bethlehem Steel were recorded in the Natural Reaction column, and the next day, May 18th, the price of U. S. Steel was recorded in the Downward Trend column. Refer to Explanatory Rule 6-D. The next day, May 19th, a red line was drawn under the Downward Trend column in Bethlehem Steel, meaning a price was made that was the same as the last price recorded in the Downward Trend column.

On May 25th, prices of U. S. Steel and Bethlehem Steel were recorded in the Secondary Rally column. Refer to Explanatory Rule 6-C.

# CHART TEN

| | SECONDARY RALLY | NATURAL RALLY | UPWARD TREND | DOWNWARD TREND | NATURAL REACTION | SECONDARY REACTION | SECONDARY RALLY | NATURAL RALLY | UPWARD TREND | DOWNWARD TREND | NATURAL REACTION | SECONDARY REACTION | SECONDARY RALLY | NATURAL RALLY | UPWARD TREND | DOWNWARD TREND | NATURAL REACTION | SECONDARY REACTION |
|---|---|---|---|---|---|---|---|---|---|---|---|---|---|---|---|---|---|---|
| | | | | 44 3/8 | | | | | | 51 5/8 | | | | | | 96 | | |
| 1939 | | 50 | | | | | | 58 1/2 | | | | | | 103 1/2 | | | | |
| DATE | | | U.S. STEEL | | | | | | BETHLEHEM STEEL | | | | | | KEY PRICE | | | |
| APR 20 | | | | | | | | | | | | | | | | | | |
| 21 | | | | | | | | | | | | | | | | | | |
| SAT. 22 | | | | | | | | | | | | | | | | | | |
| 24 | | | | | | | | | | | | | | | | | | |
| 25 | | | | | | | | | | | | | | | | | | |
| 26 | | | | | | | | | | | | | | | | | | |
| 27 | | | | | | | | | | | | | | | | | | |
| 28 | | | | | | | | | | | | | | | | | | |
| SAT. 29 | | | | | | | | | | | | | | | | | | |
| MAY 1 | | | | | | | | | | | | | | | | | | |
| 2 | | | | | | | | | | | | | | | | | | |
| 3 | | | | | | | | | | | | | | | | | | |
| 4 | | | | | | | | | | | | | | | | | | |
| 5 | | | | | | | | | | | | | | | | | | |
| SAT. 6 | | | | | | | | | | | | | | | | | | |
| 8 | | | | | | | | | | | | | | | | | | |
| 9 | | | | | | | | | | | | | | | | | | |
| 10 | | | | | | | | | | | | | | | | | | |
| 11 | | | | | | | | | | | | | | | | | | |
| 12 | | | | | | | | | | | | | | | | | | |
| SAT. 13 | | | | | | | | | | | | | | | | | | |
| 15 | | | | | | | | | | | | | | | | | | |
| 16 | | | | | | | | | | | | | | | | | | |
| 17 | | | | | 44 5/8 | | | | | | 52 | | | | | | 96 5/8 | |
| 18 | | | | 43 1/4 | | | | | | | | | | | | 95 1/4 | | |
| 19 | | | | | | | | | | | | | | | | 94 7/8 | | |
| SAT. 20 | | | | | | | | | | | | | | | | | | |
| 22 | | | | | | | | | | | | | | | | | | |
| 23 | | | | | | | | | | | | | | | | | | |
| 24 | | | | | | | | | | | | | | | | | | |
| 25 | 48 3/4 | | | | | | 57 3/4 | | | | | | 106 1/2 | | | | | |
| 26 | 49 | | | | | | 58 | | | | | | 107 | | | | | |
| SAT. 27 | 49 3/8 | | | | | | | — | | | | | 107 7/8 | | | | | |
| 29 | | 50 1/4 | | | | | | 59 3/8 | | | | | | 109 5/8 | | | | |
| 31 | | 50 7/8 | | | | | | 60 | | | | | | 110 7/8 | | | | |
| JUNE 1 | | | | | | | | | | | | | | | | | | |

On June 16th, the price of Bethlehem Steel was recorded in the Natural Reaction column. Refer to Explanatory Rule 6-B.

On June 28th, the price of U. S. Steel was recorded in the Natural Reaction column. Refer to Explanatory Rule 6-B.

On June 29th, the price of Bethlehem Steel was recorded in the Downward Trend column, being a price lower than the last price recorded in the Downward Trend column.

On July 13th, prices of U. S. Steel and Bethlehem Steel were recorded in the Secondary Rally column. Refer to Explanatory Rule 6-G.

# CHART ELEVEN

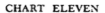

| DATE | SECONDARY RALLY | NATURAL RALLY | UPWARD TREND | DOWNWARD TREND | NATURAL REACTION | SECONDARY REACTION | SECONDARY RALLY | NATURAL RALLY | UPWARD TREND | DOWNWARD TREND | NATURAL REACTION | SECONDARY REACTION | SECONDARY RALLY | NATURAL RALLY | UPWARD TREND | DOWNWARD TREND | NATURAL REACTION | SECONDARY REACTION |
|---|---|---|---|---|---|---|---|---|---|---|---|---|---|---|---|---|---|---|
| | | | | 44 1/8 | | | | | | 51 5/8 | | | | | | 96 | | |
| | | 50 | | | | | | 58 1/2 | | | | | | 108 1/2 | | | | |
| | | | | 43 1/2 | | | | | | — | | | | | | 94 7/8 | | |
| 1939 | | 50 7/8 | | | | | | 60 | | | | | | 110 7/8 | | | | |
| DATE | | U.S. STEEL | | | | | | BETHLEHEM STEEL | | | | | | KEY PRICE | | | | |
| JUNE 2 | | | | | | | | | | | | | | | | | | |
| SAT 3 | | | | | | | | | | | | | | | | | | |
| 5 | | | | | | | | | | | | | | | | | | |
| 6 | | | | | | | | | | | | | | | | | | |
| 7 | | | | | | | | | | | | | | | | | | |
| 8 | | | | | | | | | | | | | | | | | | |
| 9 | | | | | | | | | | | | | | | | | | |
| SAT 10 | | | | | | | | | | | | | | | | | | |
| 12 | | | | | | | | | | | | | | | | | | |
| 13 | | | | | | | | | | | | | | | | | | |
| 14 | | | | | | | | | | | | | | | | | | |
| 15 | | | | | | | | | | | | | | | | | | |
| 16 | | | | | | | | | | | 54 | | | | | | | | |
| SAT 17 | | | | | | | | | | | | | | | | | | |
| 19 | | | | | | | | | | | | | | | | | | |
| 20 | | | | | | | | | | | | | | | | | | |
| 21 | | | | | | | | | | | | | | | | | | |
| 22 | | | | | | | | | | | | | | | | | | |
| 23 | | | | | | | | | | | | | | | | | | |
| SAT 24 | | | | | | | | | | | | | | | | | | |
| 26 | | | | | | | | | | | | | | | | | | |
| 27 | | | | | | | | | | | | | | | | | | |
| 28 | | | | 45 | | | | | | 52 1/2 | | | | | | 97 1/2 | | |
| 29 | | | | 43 3/4 | | | | | 51 | | | | | | | 94 3/4 | | |
| 30 | | | | 43 5/8 | | | | | 50 1/4 | | | | | | | 93 7/8 | | |
| SAT JULY 1 | | | | | | | | | | | | | | | | | | |
| 3 | | | | | | | | | | | | | | | | | | |
| 5 | | | | | | | | | | | | | | | | | | |
| 6 | | | | | | | | | | | | | | | | | | |
| 7 | | | | | | | | | | | | | | | | | | |
| SAT 8 | | | | | | | | | | | | | | | | | | |
| 10 | | | | | | | | | | | | | | | | | | |
| 11 | | | | | | | | | | | | | | | | | | |
| 12 | | | | | | | | | | | | | | | | | | |
| 13 | 48 1/4 | | | | | | 57 1/4 | | | | | | 105 1/2 | | | | | |
| 14 | | | | | | | | | | | | | | | | | | |

On July 21st, the price of Bethlehem Steel was recorded in the Upward Trend column, and the next day, July 22nd, the price of U. S. Steel was recorded in the Upward Trend column. Refer to Explanatory Rule 5-A.

On August 4th, prices of U. S. Steel and Bethlehem Steel were recorded in the Natural Reaction column. Refer to Explanatory Rule 4-A.

On August 23rd, the price of U. S. Steel was recorded in the Downward Trend column, being lower than the price previously recorded in the Downward Trend column.

# CHART TWELVE

| | SECONDARY RALLY | NATURAL RALLY | UPWARD TREND | DOWNWARD TREND | NATURAL REACTION | SECONDARY REACTION | SECONDARY RALLY | NATURAL RALLY | UPWARD TREND | DOWNWARD TREND | NATURAL REACTION | SECONDARY REACTION | SECONDARY RALLY | NATURAL RALLY | UPWARD TREND | DOWNWARD TREND | NATURAL REACTION | SECONDARY REACTION |
|---|---|---|---|---|---|---|---|---|---|---|---|---|---|---|---|---|---|---|
| | | | | 43 3/4 | | | | | | 51 5/8 | | | | | | 94 7/8 | | |
| | | 50 7/8 | | | | | | 60 | | | | | | 110 7/8 | | | | |
| | | | | | 43 5/8 | | | | | 50 1/4 | | | | | | 93 7/8 | | |
| | | | | | | | | | | | | | | | | | | |
| 1939 | 48 1/4 | | | | | | 57 1/4 | | | | | | 105 1/2 | | | | | |
| DATE | | | U.S. STEEL | | | | | | BETHLEHEM STEEL | | | | | | KEY PRICE | | | |
| SAT. JULY 15 | | | | | | | | | | | | | | | | | | |
| 17 | 50 3/4 | | | | | | | 60 3/8 | | | | | | 111 1/8 | | | | |
| 18 | | 51 7/8 | | | | | | 62 | | | | | | 113 7/8 | | | | |
| 19 | | | | | | | | | | | | | | | | | | |
| 20 | | | | | | | | | | | | | | | | | | |
| 21 | | 52 1/2 | | | | | | | 63 | | | | | 115 1/2 | | | | |
| SAT. 22 | | | 54 1/8 | | | | | | 65 | | | | | | 119 1/8 | | | |
| 24 | | | | | | | | | | | | | | | | | | |
| 25 | | | 55 1/8 | | | | | | 65 3/4 | | | | | | 120 7/8 | | | |
| 26 | | | | | | | | | | | | | | | | | | |
| 27 | | | | | | | | | | | | | | | | | | |
| 28 | | | | | | | | | | | | | | | | | | |
| SAT. 29 | | | | | | | | | | | | | | | | | | |
| 31 | | | | | | | | | | | | | | | | | | |
| AUG. 1 | | | | | | | | | | | | | | | | | | |
| 2 | | | | | | | | | | | | | | | | | | |
| 3 | | | | | | | | | | | | | | | | | | |
| 4 | | | | | 49 1/2 | | | | | | 59 1/2 | | | | | | 109 | |
| SAT. 5 | | | | | | | | | | | | | | | | | | |
| 7 | | | | | 49 1/4 | | | | | | | | | | | | 108 3/4 | |
| 8 | | | | | | | | | | | | | | | | | | |
| 9 | | | | | | | | | | | 59 | | | | | | 108 1/4 | |
| 10 | | | | | 47 3/4 | | | | | | 58 | | | | | | 105 3/4 | |
| 11 | | | | | 47 | | | | | | | | | | | | 105 | |
| SAT. 12 | | | | | | | | | | | | | | | | | | |
| 14 | | | | | | | | | | | | | | | | | | |
| 15 | | | | | | | | | | | | | | | | | | |
| 16 | | | | | | | | | | | | | | | | | | |
| 17 | | | | | 46 1/2 | | | | | | | | | | | | 104 1/2 | |
| 18 | | | | | 45 | | | | | | 55 1/8 | | | | | | 100 1/8 | |
| SAT. 19 | | | | | | | | | | | | | | | | | | |
| 21 | | | | | 43 3/8 | | | | | | 53 3/8 | | | | | | 96 3/4 | |
| 22 | | | | | | | | | | | | | | | | | | |
| 23 | | | | 42 5/8 | | | | | | | | | | | | | 96 | |
| 24 | | | | 41 5/8 | | | | | | | 51 7/8 | | | | | 93 1/2 | | |
| 25 | | | | | | | | | | | | | | | | | | |

On August 29th, prices of U. S. Steel and Bethlehem Steel were recorded in the Natural Rally column. Refer to Explanatory Rule 6-D.

On September 2nd, prices of U. S. Steel and Bethlehem Steel were recorded in the Upward Trend column, being higher prices than the last prices previously recorded in the Upward Trend column.

On September 14th, prices of U. S. Steel and Bethlehem Steel were recorded in the Natural Reaction column. Refer to Explanatory Rules 6-A and 4-A.

On September 19th, prices of U. S. Steel and Bethlehem Steel were recorded in the Natural Rally column. Refer to Explanatory Rules 6-D and 4-B.

On September 28th, prices for U. S. Steel and Bethlehem Steel were recorded in the Secondary Reaction column. Refer to Explanatory Rule 6-H.

On October 6th, prices of U. S. Steel and Bethlehem Steel were recorded in the Secondary Rally column. Refer to Explanatory Rule 6-G.

# CHART THIRTEEN

| | SECONDARY RALLY | NATURAL RALLY | UPWARD TREND | DOWNWARD TREND | NATURAL REACTION | SECONDARY REACTION | SECONDARY RALLY | NATURAL RALLY | UPWARD TREND | DOWNWARD TREND | NATURAL REACTION | SECONDARY REACTION | SECONDARY RALLY | NATURAL RALLY | UPWARD TREND | DOWNWARD TREND | NATURAL REACTION | SECONDARY REACTION |
|---|---|---|---|---|---|---|---|---|---|---|---|---|---|---|---|---|---|---|
| | | | | 43 1/4 | | | | | | 50 1/4 | | | | | | 93 7/8 | | |
| | | | 55 1/8 | | | | | | 65 3/4 | | | | | | 120 7/8 | | | |
| | | | | | | | | | | | | | | | | | | |
| 1939 | | | | 41 5/8 | | | | | | | 51 7/8 | | | | | 93 1/2 | | |
| DATE | | | U.S. STEEL | | | | | | BETHLEHEM STEEL | | | | | | KEY PRICE | | | |
| SAT. AUG. 26 | | | | | | | | | | | | | | | | | | |
| 28 | | | | | | | | | | | | | | | | | | |
| 29 | | 48 | | | | | | 60 1/2 | | | | | | 108 1/2 | | | | |
| 30 | | | | | | | | | | | | | | | | | | |
| 31 | | | | | | | | | | | | | | | | | | |
| SEPT. 1 | | 52 | | | | | | 65 1/2 | | | | | | 117 1/2 | | | | |
| SAT 2 | | | 55 1/4 | | | | | | 70 3/8 | | | | | | 125 5/8 | | | |
| 5 | | | 66 7/8 | | | | | | 85 1/2 | | | | | | 152 3/8 | | | |
| 6 | | | | | | | | | | | | | | | | | | |
| 7 | | | | | | | | | | | | | | | | | | |
| 8 | | | 69 3/4 | | | | | | 87 | | | | | | 156 3/4 | | | |
| SAT. 9 | | | 70 | | | | | | 88 3/4 | | | | | | 158 3/4 | | | |
| 11 | | | 78 5/8 | | | | | | 100 | | | | | | 178 5/8 | | | |
| 12 | | | 82 3/4 | | | | | | | | | | | | 182 3/4 | | | |
| 13 | | | | | | | | | | | | | | | | | | |
| 14 | | | | | 76 3/8 | | | | | | 91 3/4 | | | | | | 168 1/8 | |
| 15 | | | | | | | | | | | | | | | | | | |
| SAT 16 | | | | | 75 1/2 | | | | | | 88 3/8 | | | | | | 163 7/8 | |
| 18 | | | | | 70 1/2 | | | | | | 83 3/4 | | | | | | 154 1/4 | |
| 19 | | 78 | | | | | | 92 3/8 | | | | | | 170 3/8 | | | | |
| 20 | | 80 5/8 | | | | | | 95 5/8 | | | | | | 176 1/4 | | | | |
| 21 | | | | | | | | | | | | | | | | | | |
| 22 | | | | | | | | | | | | | | | | | | |
| SAT 23 | | | | | | | | | | | | | | | | | | |
| 25 | | | | | | | | | | | | | | | | | | |
| 26 | | | | | | | | | | | | | | | | | | |
| 27 | | | | | | | | | | | | | | | | | | |
| 28 | | | | | | 75 1/8 | | | | | | 89 | | | | | | 164 1/8 |
| 29 | | | | | | 73 1/2 | | | | | | 86 3/4 | | | | | | 160 1/4 |
| SAT 30 | | | | | | | | | | | | | | | | | | |
| OCT. 2 | | | | | | | | | | | | | | | | | | |
| 3 | | | | | | | | | | | | | | | | | | |
| 4 | | | | | | 73 | | | | | | 86 1/4 | | | | | | 159 1/4 |
| 5 | | | | | | | | | | | | | | | | | | |
| 6 | 78 1/2 | | | | | | 92 3/4 | | | | | | 171 1/4 | | | | | |
| SAT. 7 | | | | | | | | | | | | | | | | | | |

On November 3rd, the price of U. S. Steel was recorded in the Secondary Reaction column, being a price lower than the last previous price recorded in that column.

On November 9th, a dash was made in the Natural Reaction column of U. S. Steel, being the same price that was last recorded in the Natural Reaction column, and on the same day a new price was recorded in the Natural Reaction column of Bethlehem Steel, being a lower price than the last price previously recorded in that column.

# CHART FOURTEEN

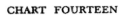

Column groups: **U.S. STEEL** (columns 1–6), **BETHLEHEM STEEL** (columns 7–12), **KEY PRICE** (columns 13–18). Each group has the columns: SECONDARY RALLY · NATURAL RALLY · UPWARD TREND · DOWNWARD TREND · NATURAL REACTION · SECONDARY REACTION.

| DATE | SEC. RALLY | NAT. RALLY | UPWARD TREND | DOWNWARD TREND | NAT. REACTION | SEC. REACTION | SEC. RALLY | NAT. RALLY | UPWARD TREND | DOWNWARD TREND | NAT. REACTION | SEC. REACTION | SEC. RALLY | NAT. RALLY | UPWARD TREND | DOWNWARD TREND | NAT. REACTION | SEC. REACTION |
|---|---|---|---|---|---|---|---|---|---|---|---|---|---|---|---|---|---|---|
| | | | $92\frac{3}{4}$ | | | | | | 100 | | | | | | $182\frac{3}{4}$ | | | |
| | | | | $79\frac{1}{2}$ | | | | | | $83\frac{3}{4}$ | | | | | | | $159\frac{1}{4}$ | |
| | | $80\frac{5}{8}$ | | | | | $95\frac{5}{8}$ | | | | | | | $176\frac{1}{4}$ | | | | |
| | | | | | 73 | | | | | | $86\frac{1}{4}$ | | | | | | | $159\frac{1}{4}$ |
| 1939 | $78\frac{1}{2}$ | | | | | $92\frac{3}{4}$ | | | | | | | $171\frac{1}{4}$ | | | | | |
| OCT. 9 | | | | | | | | | | | | | | | | | | |
| 10 | | | | | | | | | | | | | | | | | | |
| 11 | | | | | | | | | | | | | | | | | | |
| 13 | | | | | | | | | | | | | | | | | | |
| SAT. 14 | | | | | | | | | | | | | | | | | | |
| 16 | | | | | | | | | | | | | | | | | | |
| 17 | $78\frac{7}{8}$ | | | | | $93\frac{7}{8}$ | | | | | | | $172\frac{3}{4}$ | | | | | |
| 18 | $79\frac{1}{4}$ | | | | | | | | | | | | $173\frac{1}{2}$ | | | | | |
| 19 | | | | | | | | | | | | | | | | | | |
| 20 | | | | | | | | | | | | | | | | | | |
| SAT. 21 | | | | | | | | | | | | | | | | | | |
| 23 | | | | | | | | | | | | | | | | | | |
| 24 | | | | | | | | | | | | | | | | | | |
| 25 | | | | | | | | | | | | | | | | | | |
| 26 | | | | | | | | | | | | | | | | | | |
| 27 | | | | | | | | | | | | | | | | | | |
| SAT. 28 | | | | | | | | | | | | | | | | | | |
| 30 | | | | | | | | | | | | | | | | | | |
| 31 | | | | | | | | | | | | | | | | | | |
| NOV. 1 | | | | | | | | | | | | | | | | | | |
| 2 | | | | | | | | | | | | | | | | | | |
| 3 | | | | | $72\frac{1}{2}$ | | | | | | | | | | | | | | |
| SAT. 4 | | | | | | | | | | | | | | | | | | |
| 6 | | | | | | | | | | | | | | | | | | |
| 8 | | | | | $72\frac{1}{8}$ | | | | | | | $86\frac{1}{8}$ | | | | | | | $158\frac{1}{4}$ |
| 9 | | | | — | | | | | | | $83\frac{1}{4}$ | | | | | | | $153\frac{3}{4}$ | |
| 10 | | | | $63\frac{3}{4}$ | | | | | | | $81\frac{3}{8}$ | | | | | | | $150\frac{1}{2}$ | |
| 13 | | | | | | | | | | | | | | | | | | |
| 14 | | | | | | | | | | | | | | | | | | |
| 15 | | | | | | | | | | | | | | | | | | |
| 16 | | | | | | | | | | | | | | | | | | |
| 17 | | | | | | | | | | | | | | | | | | |
| SAT. 18 | | | | | | | | | | | | | | | | | | |
| 20 | | | | | | | | | | | | | | | | | | |
| 21 | | | | | | | | | | | | | | | | | | |
| 22 | | | | | | | | | | | | | | | | | | |

On November 24th, the price of U. S. Steel was recorded in the Downward Trend column. Refer to Explanatory Rule 6-E, and the next day, November 25th, the price of Bethlehem Steel was recorded in the Downward Trend column. Refer to Explanatory Rule 6-E.

On December 7th, prices of U. S. Steel and Bethlehem Steel were recorded in the Natural Rally column. Refer to Explanatory Rule 6-C.

## CHART FIFTEEN

| | SECONDARY RALLY | NATURAL RALLY | UPWARD TREND | DOWNWARD TREND | NATURAL REACTION | SECONDARY REACTION | SECONDARY RALLY | NATURAL RALLY | UPWARD TREND | DOWNWARD TREND | NATURAL REACTION | SECONDARY REACTION | SECONDARY RALLY | NATURAL RALLY | UPWARD TREND | DOWNWARD TREND | NATURAL REACTION | SECONDARY REACTION |
|---|---|---|---|---|---|---|---|---|---|---|---|---|---|---|---|---|---|---|
| | | | 82 3/4 | | | | | | 100 | | | | | | 182 5/8 | | | |
| | | | | | 70 1/2 | | | | | | 83 3/4 | | | | | | 154 1/4 | |
| | | 80 5/8 | | | | | | 95 5/8 | | | | | | 176 1/4 | | | | |
| | | | | | | | | | | | | | | | | | | |
| 1939 | | | | | 68 3/4 | | | | | | 81 3/4 | | | | | | 150 1/2 | |
| DATE | | | U.S. STEEL | | | | | | BETHLEHEM STEEL | | | | | | KEY PRICE | | | |
| NOV. 24 | | | | 66 7/8 | | | | | | | 81 | | | | | 147 7/8 | | |
| SAT. 25 | | | | | | | | | | 80 3/4 | | | | | | 147 5/8 | | |
| 27 | | | | | | | | | | | | | | | | | | |
| 28 | | | | | | | | | | | | | | | | | | |
| 29 | | | | 65 7/8 | | | | | | 78 1/8 | | | | | | 144 | | |
| 30 | | | | 63 5/8 | | | | | | 77 | | | | | | 140 5/8 | | |
| DEC. 1 | | | | | | | | | | | | | | | | | | |
| SAT. 2 | | | | | | | | | | | | | | | | | | |
| 4 | | | | | | | | | | | | | | | | | | |
| 5 | | | | | | | | | | | | | | | | | | |
| 6 | | | | | | | | | | | | | | | | | | |
| 7 | | 69 3/4 | | | | | | 84 | | | | | | 153 3/4 | | | | |
| 8 | | | | | | | | | | | | | | | | | | |
| SAT. 9 | | | | | | | | | | | | | | | | | | |
| 11 | | | | | | | | | | | | | | | | | | |
| 12 | | | | | | | | | | | | | | | | | | |
| 13 | | | | | | | | | | | | | | | | | | |
| 14 | | | | | | | | 84 7/8 | | | | | | 154 5/8 | | | | |
| 15 | | | | | | | | | | | | | | | | | | |
| SAT. 16 | | | | | | | | | | | | | | | | | | |
| 18 | | | | | | | | | | | | | | | | | | |
| 19 | | | | | | | | | | | | | | | | | | |
| 20 | | | | | | | | | | | | | | | | | | |
| 21 | | | | | | | | | | | | | | | | | | |
| 22 | | | | | | | | | | | | | | | | | | |
| SAT 23 | | | | | | | | | | | | | | | | | | |
| 26 | | | | | | | | | | | | | | | | | | |
| 27 | | | | | | | | | | | | | | | | | | |
| 28 | | | | | | | | | | | | | | | | | | |
| 29 | | | | | | | | | | | | | | | | | | |
| SAT. 30 | | | | | | | | | | | | | | | | | | |
| 1940 JAN. 2 | | | | | | | | | | | | | | | | | | |
| 3 | | | | | | | | | | | | | | | | | | |
| 4 | | | | | | | | | | | | | | | | | | |
| 5 | | | | | | | | | | | | | | | | | | |
| SAT 6 | | | | | | | | | | | | | | | | | | |

On January 9th, prices of U. S. Steel and Bethlehem Steel were recorded in the Natural Reaction column. Refer to Explanatory Rule 6-B.

On January 11th, prices of U. S. Steel and Bethlehem Steel were recorded in the Downward Trend column, being prices lower than the last recorded prices in the Downward Trend columns.

On February 7th, prices are recorded in the Natural Rally column of Bethlehem Steel, this being the first day it rallied the required distance of six points. The following day U. S. Steel is recorded in addition to Bethlehem Steel and the Key Price, the latter having rallied the proper distance to be used in recording.

# CHART SIXTEEN

| Date | SECONDARY RALLY | NATURAL RALLY | UPWARD TREND | DOWNWARD TREND | NATURAL REACTION | SECONDARY REACTION | SECONDARY RALLY | NATURAL RALLY | UPWARD TREND | DOWNWARD TREND | NATURAL REACTION | SECONDARY REACTION | SECONDARY RALLY | NATURAL RALLY | UPWARD TREND | DOWNWARD TREND | NATURAL REACTION | SECONDARY REACTION |
|---|---|---|---|---|---|---|---|---|---|---|---|---|---|---|---|---|---|---|
| | | | | $63\frac{5}{8}$ | | | | | | 77 | | | | | | $140\frac{5}{8}$ | | |
| 1940 | | $69\frac{3}{4}$ | | | | | | $84\frac{7}{8}$ | | | | | | $154\frac{5}{8}$ | | | | |
| | | | *U.S. STEEL* | | | | | *BETHLEHEM STEEL* | | | | | | | *KEY PRICE* | | | |
| JAN 8 | | | | | | | | | | | | | | | | | | |
| 9 | | | | $64\frac{1}{4}$ | | | | | | $78\frac{1}{2}$ | | | | | | $142\frac{3}{4}$ | | |
| 10 | | | | $63\frac{3}{4}$ | | | | | | | | | | | | $142\frac{1}{4}$ | | |
| 11 | | | | 62 | | | | | | $76\frac{1}{2}$ | | | | | | $138\frac{1}{2}$ | | |
| 12 | | | | $60\frac{1}{8}$ | | | | | | $74\frac{7}{8}$ | | | | | | $134\frac{1}{4}$ | | |
| SAT 13 | | | | $59\frac{5}{8}$ | | | | | | $73\frac{1}{2}$ | | | | | | $133\frac{3}{8}$ | | |
| 15 | | | | $57\frac{1}{2}$ | | | | | | 72 | | | | | | $129\frac{1}{2}$ | | |
| 16 | | | | | | | | | | | | | | | | | | |
| 17 | | | | | | | | | | | | | | | | | | |
| 18 | | | | $56\frac{7}{8}$ | | | | | | $71\frac{1}{2}$ | | | | | | $128\frac{3}{8}$ | | |
| 19 | | | | | | | | | | 71 | | | | | | $127\frac{7}{8}$ | | |
| SAT 20 | | | | | | | | | | | | | | | | | | |
| 22 | | | | $55\frac{3}{8}$ | | | | | | $70\frac{1}{8}$ | | | | | | 126 | | |
| 23 | | | | | | | | | | | | | | | | | | |
| 24 | | | | | | | | | | | | | | | | | | |
| 25 | | | | | | | | | | | | | | | | | | |
| 26 | | | | | | | | | | | | | | | | | | |
| SAT 27 | | | | | | | | | | | | | | | | | | |
| 29 | | | | | | | | | | | | | | | | | | |
| 30 | | | | | | | | | | | | | | | | | | |
| 31 | | | | | | | | | | | | | | | | | | |
| FEB 1 | | | | | | | | | | | | | | | | | | |
| 2 | | | | | | | | | | | | | | | | | | |
| SAT 3 | | | | | | | | | | | | | | | | | | |
| 5 | | | | | | | | | | | | | | | | | | |
| 6 | | | | | | | | | | | | | | | | | | |
| 7 | | | | | | | | $76\frac{3}{8}$ | | | | | | | | | | |
| 8 | | 61 | | | | | | 78 | | | | | | 139 | | | | |
| 9 | | $61\frac{3}{4}$ | | | | | | $79\frac{1}{2}$ | | | | | | $141\frac{1}{2}$ | | | | |
| SAT 10 | | | | | | | | | | | | | | | | | | |
| 13 | | | | | | | | | | | | | | | | | | |
| 14 | | | | | | | | | | | | | | | | | | |
| 15 | | | | | | | | | | | | | | | | | | |
| 16 | | | | $56\frac{1}{8}$ | | | | | | | | | | | | | | |
| SAT 17 | | | | | | | | | | | | | | | | | | |
| 19 | | | | | | | | | | | | | | | | | | |